JAPANESE INTERFIRM NETWORKS AND THEIR MAIN BANKS

Japanese Interfirm Networks and Their Main Banks

Mark J. Scher

First published in Great Britain 1997 by
MACMILLAN PRESS LTD
Houndmills, Basingstoke, Hampshire RG21 6XS and London
Companies and representatives throughout the world

A catalogue record for this book is available from the British Library.

ISBN 0–333–71965–4

First published in the United States of America 1997 by
ST. MARTIN'S PRESS, INC.,
Scholarly and Reference Division,
175 Fifth Avenue, New York, N.Y. 10010

ISBN 0–312–17743–7

Library of Congress Cataloging-in-Publication Data
Scher, Mark J.
Japanese interfirm networks and their main banks / by Mark J.
Scher.
p. cm.
Includes bibliographical references and index.
ISBN 0–312–17743–7 (cloth)
1. Business networks—Japan.   2. Banks and banking—Japan.
I. Title.
HD69.S8S328 1998
332.1'6—dc21   97–24723
                                                                        CIP

This book is printed on paper suitable for recycling and made from fully managed and sustained forest sources.

10   9   8   7   6   5   4   3   2   1
06   05   04   03   02   01   00   99   98   97

Printed and bound in Great Britain by
Antony Rowe Ltd, Chippenham, Wiltshire

To **Ann**, at XXX,
without whose help and support this book,
and all of my life's work,
would not have been possible.

Contents

List of Figures and Tables

Figures

Tables

Acknowledgments

The idea for this book began in Manchester, England, in 1992 and took shape in Tokyo and New York thanks to the aid and comfort of many generous-spirited people who shared with me their ideas, their opinions, their time, and their hospitality.

First, I express my profound gratitude to all of the Japanese banking practitioners who, with much patience, allowed me the privilege and the time to meet and get to know them. I regret that discretion requires their names and institutions remain anonymous. Clearly, their views and experiences form the core of this book.

I am most grateful to Tokyo Keizai University, where I was Visiting Research Fellow during the field research for this book. I am particularly indebted to Yoshiaki Jinnai, the members of the Accounting Faculty Seminar, Shigekazu Kukita, Tomoko Taka-yama, and Akiyoshi Tanaka, who became my good friends and good critics. I thank as well the library and support staff of Tokyo Keizai, Atsumu Hosoi, Toru Sasaki, and Tamiko Kimura. As a result of their many kindnesses, Tokyo Keizai was indeed a home away from home.

As this book was a work-in-progress for several years, a number of scholars took time out of their crowded schedules to comment on earlier portions of this book. I am honored to be able to thank Akiyoshi Horiuchi for his continuing encouragement of my research over the years. I also thank the following scholars for their comments and criticisms of earlier drafts: Shoichi Asajima, Max Boisot, Tamio Hattori, Geert Hofstede, Chie Nakane, Hiroshi Okumura, Hugh Patrick, C. Tait Ratcliffe, Juro Teranishi, and Adrian Tschoegl.

I am also indebted to the following scholars for their good advice: Dick Beason, Schon Beechler, Abito Itoh, Yoichi Kawanami, Takase Kyosuke, Cheryl Lehman, Dale Littler, Tadashi Mito, Hideaki Miyajima, Tetsuji Okazaki, Paul Sheard, Tony Tinker, Kazuo Ueda, and Hideo Ueki.

Two research studies on Japanese firms enabled me to triangulate my bank-side data. I benefited greatly from extensive discussions with Osamu Kikuchi, principal researcher of the Fuji Sogo

xi

Kenkyujo study, and with Kei'ichi Omura, chief author of the Keiei Academy Report.

At the Manchester School of Management, thanks go to Penny Ciancanelli, my supervisor; Ken Green, advisor and director of the doctoral program who helped me survive my mid-life Ph.D. crisis; David Knights, internal examiner of my thesis; and Brian McCormick of the University of Sheffield, my external examiner. Their individual and collective wisdom helped shape my thesis and ultimately this book.

I am extremely appreciative of the generously given assistance of my colleagues, present and past, at the Institute for Financial Affairs, Takashi Yoshinaga, Haruo Tanigawa, and Alla Yarin.

In addition, I extend my sincere thanks to the following organizations: The European Management and Organizations in Transition (EMOT) Workshops, from which I received support from the European Science Foundation in Barcelona (1996) and Turin (1996). I particularly thank discussants Franz Traxler and Behlul Usdiken for their insightful comments as well as my fellow workshop participants. I also thank fellow participants of the European Group for Organizational Studies (EGOS) Colloquium in Istanbul (1995).

Portions of this book were presented as papers at the annual meetings of the Association for Japanese Business Studies: New York (1993), Vancouver (1994), Ann Arbor (1995), and the Academy of International Business annual meetings in Maui (1993), Seoul (1995), and Banff (1996). I was most fortunate at those times to have the benefit of the comments of Ed Duerr, Michael Smitka, Allan Bird, and Tom Roehl as discussants.

I am deeply indebted to family and friends Yukio and Mire Miyazaki, Chuhei Sugiyama, Yasuko Jinnai, Kaori Kuroda, Masaya Fujita, and John Yoxall for their unfailing and unstinting friendship and support during the long process of researching this book.

I have reserved these last words of acknowledgment for Takashi Fujimoto, Setsu Kamiyama, and Yoshiaki Jinnai, whose help and guidance helped me bridge cultures and generations. I thank them not only for their considerable assistance but the lengths to which they extended their friendship.

Although I benefited from the assistance of a great many people in writing this book, I claim all of its shortcomings as my own.

MARK J. SCHER

1 Introduction and Overview

POLICY IMPLICATIONS

In 1992, when the research for this book began, many in the popular press, business media, and academicians were enthusiastically describing Japanese industrial groups, the so-called "keiretsu," and the main bank system, not only as the keys to Japan's great postwar recovery, but also as superior forms of industrial and financial organization [Nakatani, 1984, 1990; Imai, 1990] that could and should be emulated by the lagging economies of the industrialized world. Indeed, the Japanese main bank system was being advocated in studies by such institutions as the World Bank as a model for economic development for the former socialist countries of Eastern Europe and the newly emerging economies of the developing world [Aoki and Patrick, 1994]. Similarly, a body of management-oriented literature was developing which argued that the formation of Japanese-style industrial groups could and should be implemented elsewhere, implicitly presuming that this organizational structure is available to U.S. and European managers simply as a policy choice [see for example: Ferguson, 1990; *Harvard Business Review*, 1990; *Business Week*, 1992; Burt and Doyle, 1993].

At the same time that Japanese industrial groups and their main bank system were being hailed as exemplars of economic and managerial efficiency, they had also become the subject of bitter contention in the U.S.–Japan trade talks. At the center of the debate were issues relating to the lack of "access" to Japan's industrial and financial markets and Japanese exclusive, if not collusive, trade practices [see for example: Okumura 1990a, 1991, 1993, among others]. Interfirm relations among Japanese companies were condemned by U.S. negotiators for all but locking out competitors, both foreign and domestic.

1

The Japanese negotiating side found justification for its positions in the growing lore and literature advocating the Japanese system. This viewpoint extolled the superiority of bank-centered financing for industrial development, theorizing a highly stylized model of Japanese governance structures that was built around the Japanese main bank system. This model described the benevolent corporate synergism of the Japanese form of industrial organization, where even cross-shareholding was portrayed as "meritorious" [Japan Economic Planning Agency, 1992].

It was in the shadow of this debate on Japanese governance structures that I began a four-year research project on the relationship between main banks and their client firms. This research ultimately tested the most basic assumptions made about the main bank system and its purported governance role, assumptions which formed the keystone of the agency economists' model, particularly in regard to: (1) efficiencies of capital derived from the delegated cost of monitoring, the so-called signal function; (2) main bank assistance to firms in financial distress, the so-called rescue function; (3) the main bank role in corporate governance.

The importance of governance issues had already come to the forefront of Japanese concern as a result of a confluence of foreign and domestic pressures. International trade negotiations had focused Japanese public attention on issues such as the lack of access by foreign institutions to Japan's financial markets. At the same time, the ongoing process of governmental deregulation of financial services by the Ministry of Finance had fostered fresh tensions between the banking and securities industries, particularly over the banks' newly acquired right to underwrite corporate bonds, which further increased the main bank's putative power over its client firms. By the commencement of this research, new, even more fundamental issues relating to corporate governance and the main bank system had emerged and were rapidly escalating into crisis following the collapse of the "bubble economy" of the late 1980s. The collapse had resulted in Japan's most profound recession since the postwar period, which had in turn led to grave economic consequences—the hollowing-out of Japan's domestic industrial production, boding the end of such hallowed institutions as long-term employment, and an asset inflation crisis threatening the very viability of the Japanese banking system itself.

Recently, other policy questions with corporate governance implications have also come into wide discussion in the West, relating to the nature of "trust" in interfirm relations and the network characteristics of "trust," among other things. The Japanese industrial group system has often been imputed with benevolent, self-protective characteristics involving "trust." According to this view, the firms in a *keiretsu* are tied with bonds of trust and obligation to their members. The analysis presented in this book is quite different from such interpretations which totally overlook the asymmetrical power relationships inherent in the *keiretsu* system. It is one of our conclusions that at the core of the Japanese industrial group system are complex power-based, rather than, for example, trust-based, interfirm relationships. It is only this kind of network that could have permitted the hollowing-out of industrial production in Japan, in which the *keiretsu* system was used as a distancing mechanism to create and maintain relationships *without* obligation.

One root cause for the debate over the nature of Japanese industrial groups and the main bank system comes from the fact that the very terms of the debate have been skewed by the misuse of terminology. Such words as *keiretsu*, cross-shareholding, trust, relationship and access, all of which we will discuss later in some detail, have been used in ways that obscure and confuse the issues. Our research discovered these inconsistencies, however, only after exhaustive interviews that examined the minutiae of the daily practices of the bankers' dealings with their clients. Major discrepancies in the understood meanings of basic terminology implicated the theoretical and political positions staked out by most of the major participants in the current policy debates on the nature of the so-called *keiretsu* and the main bank system. Fundamental misconceptions predicated on divergent usages of the same terms were likewise institutionalized in the ongoing U.S.–Japan trade talks. How much of this obfuscation exists by design or merely as a result of cross-cultural confusion is an open question.

In our discussion of Japan's industrial groups we introduce principles of insider-versus-outsider "relational access" that, in our view, underlie all transactions. This analysis of Japanese interfirm and industrial group relations argues that core Japanese business practices are determined by sets of uncodified rules and obligations that are opaque to outsider scrutiny. The governing principle underlying these rules and obligations is described as "relational access," a highly nuanced continuum of relationships—informal, invisible, and inescapable—by which the gradations of interfirm relations from insider to outsider are determined.

We present this framework as the Relational Access Paradigm, a three-dimensional, holistic model which encompasses the inter- and intrafirm attributes of Japanese industrial groups and their member firms. The relational access principle is described as the "*uchi–soto* (insider–outsider) continuum." Every relationship is located along the continuum, a firm's place in the continuum determining a number of things, but chiefly its degree of access to group member firms. This insider–outsider concept of access and relationship is essential to an understanding of the nature of Japanese industrial group relations, in which false assumptions as to what determines access, for example, have created serious stumbling blocks in the trade negotiations between Japan and its trading partners.

Thus, this book questions the basic assumptions that have implicitly shaped many policy issues, notably in the analysis of such outcomes as: whether Japanese industrial groups and their main bank system function to keep Japan's markets closed; whether the system functions beneficially for the economy in Japan; and whether the system is desirable or even culturally transportable to many other economies.

THE CHAPTERS: AN OVERVIEW

As anyone who is accustomed to doing research in Japan will attest, there are two contrasting versions of reality that all Japanese have to deal with, "*tatemae*" (façade) and "*honne*" (real story). *Tatemae* has its place in maintaining social cohesion with minimal friction but should never be confused with the *honne*. Getting to the *honne* requires the kind of access accorded only to an insider and generally is achievable only through the cultivation of long-term relationships. Not too surprisingly, previous research approaches often had unknowingly ended up with results based largely on *tatemae*, as was the case with many of the popular governance models.

In Chapter 2, Developing Theory from Practice: A Methodological Approach, we describe in detail our primary methodological tool, the interview of Japanese bankers, which involved extended field research over four years. We explain the development and refinement of our research method and the process of cross-validation with the contemporaneous Japanese research projects with which we consulted. This methodology implemented a demanding investigative system that not only tested its results over time but also cross-tested qualitative institutional data internally and externally and against quantitative data developed by Japanese researchers studying the firm's side of the main bank relationship. This triangulation of qualitative with quantitative data provided the evidence, first, to de-mythify a number of false assumptions contained in the existing literature which had set our initial research agenda and, second, to build our paradigm.

The field research for this book is based on extensive data drawn from multiple, in-depth interviews with the same seventy-one Japanese bank practitioner respondents over a four-year period. In the course of these interviews a considerable amount of evidence was gathered which not only challenges prior assumptions, but also provides an understanding of banking practices which underlie the main bank's relationship with its client firm. We also review and discuss the research of Japanese scholars who have explored many of these same issues relating to governance structures but whose work has gone inexplicably unnoticed by the proponents of agency theory and transaction-cost analysis, and, for that matter, by most scholars outside of Japan.

Origins of the Japanese Firm and the Western Paradigm

This book first began to take its present form when, in the course of research, it became apparent that many aspects of the main banks' relationships with their client firms predated the introduction of modern banking practices in Japan during the Meiji period of the late nineteenth century. This, in turn, raised questions about the usefulness—when applied to Japan—of the standard theories of the firm as propounded by economic theorists. In Chapter 3, Relational Access versus the Western Economic Paradigm, we present the view that our model of the Japanese firm uncovers significant deficiencies in the major universalistic theories of the firm promulgated by Western economists, namely, transaction-cost theory and agency theory. We argue that these deficiencies betray a mistaken and reductionist linearity in thinking. The approach of transaction-cost analysis represents a continuum between two opposing idealized modes—the market mode versus the hierarchical mode. The approach of agency theory typically sees the firm as a nexus of linear contracts and is rooted in the concept of a bundle of freely marketable contractual rights historically embodied in the seventeenth-century Anglo-Dutch concept of the joint-stock company. Although claiming to be universalistic theories, both the transaction-cost and agency approaches fail to account for some of the outstanding characteristics of the Japanese firm and market, such as the quite notable lack of freedom, information, and transparency, *a priori* requirements for efficient marketplace theories to be relevant, and overlook the social embeddedness of economic relations and transactions, the issues we deal with in our model.

In the first part of Chapter 3, Economic Theories of the Firm, we consider the following theories: Neoclassical; Principal–Agent; Nexus of Contracts; Commodity/Property Rights; Transaction Cost; and in the second part, what we term Communal forms of the firm, specifically the "clan" and the "fief" forms. Lastly, in the third part of the chapter, we propose our own framework, the Relational Access Paradigm, which adds the third dimension—the *uchi* (insider)–*soto* (outsider) continuum—to these two Communal forms. This dimension of graded concentric relationships, spheres of relationships that exist within sets and subsets, transforms the Communal model into a more holistic paradigm of the Japanese firm and its inter- and intragroup relations.

Our paradigm requires that the boundaries of the concept of the firm be extended beyond those drawn by *de jure* property rights theories to encompass a concept of the firm as a dynamic arena of collective action that depends for its viability as an institution on the supportive milieu in which it is situated. In this model, the Japanese firm is viewed as a nexus of *implicit relational* contracts, indicative of a high-context, communal form of industrial organization, in contradistinction to the firm as a nexus of linear contracts in a freely negotiated market.

We hold the linchpin of the Japanese form to be a graded pattern of concentric relationships which can be historically traced from the *ie*-style merchant household of pre-modern Japan to today's corporate relationships and the *kigyo shudan* and *keiretsu* industrial group forms. Within the concentric spheres, issues of ranking, relatedness, and identification as either *uchi* (insider) or *soto* (outsider) are as significant today as they were four hundred or more years ago. We propose, further, that the formation of the production unit in Japan remains fundamentally coextensive with an elaborated meaning of kinship and household, and with the loyalties and allegiances which those inspire.

In Chapter 4, Origins of the Japanese Firm and Interfirm Networks, we examine how the *ie*-system provided both the historical foundation for the development of Japanese firms as group entities and the basis for the transformation of Japanese enterprise across the centuries into the present-day forms as member firms of *kigyo shudan* and *keiretsu*. We describe the historical antecedents that prepared the way for the great trading houses and their commercial banks, known as the *zaibatsu* in the prewar period, and how their earlier "house" practices not only prefigured the relationship for the six large corporate enterprise groups *(kigyo shudan)* of today, but, more significantly, are also prototypic of the formation of relationships between industrial groups, both big and small, throughout Japanese society and its economy.

Industrial Groups and Their Main Banks

Against this backdrop we then examine in concrete detail the relationship of the Japanese main bank system to governance structures. Governance theories have yielded a different, albeit related, set of attributes, in the current discussion on industrial group relationships. These relate, principally, to the purposes of cross-held shareholding within the group and the nature of the role and responsibilities of group members, particularly the main bank. Writings on Japanese corporate governance generally locate and define the firm within the context of a group or conglomerate whose goal is to maintain a stable set of relationships within the group. Cross-shareholding relationships in business are often taken to imply a concomitant corporate governance function by which one company watchfully protects its interests in the other, so that, in this interpretation, the focus is restricted to the extent and effectiveness of cross-shareholding as a governance tool.

It is our view, however, that the actual workings of cross shareholding in Japan are clearly opposed to the generally held principles of governance insofar as corporate governance is inextricably linked to notions of accountability to shareholders and shareholder rights. In Chapter 5, Japanese Governance Structures in the Postwar Era: Industrial Groups and Their Main Banks, we analyze the meanings and ramifications of these interlocking relationships and the resurrection of industrial groups in the postwar era. We then turn to some of the principal assertions by agency theorists as to how corporate governance is effected through group membership, purportedly through the appointment of outside directors by the group's bank and monitoring by the main bank's team. In this chapter we also review and discuss the research of scholars in Japan who have explored many of the same issues, and to whom agency theorists have yet to respond.

The Main Bank Relationship: Governance or Competitive Strategy?

In Chapter 6, The Main Bank Relationship: *Tatemae* or *Honne*, "Stylized Facts" or Real Facts?, we present the qualitative evidence from our interviews and focus on issues of competitiveness and profitability as they relate to the strategic and structural needs of main banks and their client firms. In general, the literature to date has tended to emphasize the benefits of the main bank relationship to the corporate enterprise, especially in terms of the efficiency of capital or when a firm is in financial distress, as well as its benefits to the economic development of society, particularly in times of scarcity of capital. Such interpretations ignore the bank's own institutional reasons for promoting the relationship. Treating the bank as a "black box," the literature has largely overlooked how the bank itself benefits as the "main bank" of the relationship to the bank itself. This subject, at most, only implied within other analyses, is in fact central to an understanding of the actual workings of the main bank relationship.

Chapter 6 explores the nature of the main bank in its roles as major creditor and lender of last resort to its clients within banking's cultural, historical and institutional context, and in relation to governmental institutions that strive to foster economic development through the main bank system. In so doing it discloses some of the myriad formal and informal systems which the main bank uses to structure a profitable and lasting relationhip with its client firms, the nature of the direct rewards sought by the banks, and how their needs are served by the main bank relationship, namely, what the areas of real profitability are for the banks, why second and third banks in the lending hierarchy can expect the same kind of profitability, though to a lesser degree, and what the main bank relationship involves for the banks.

In Chapter 7, Bank versus Firm: Triangulating the Data, we discuss our findings regarding main bank monitoring and its purported "signal" function, and main bank governance through cross-shareholding. We also triangulate our qualitative bank interview data with the quantitative data of two Japanese research teams' surveys that studied the main bank relationship from the client firm's perspective, and we apply the results to our own model based on the *uchi–soto* continuum and the main bank relationship.

CONCLUSIONS IN BRIEF

Many Japanese banking practices can be better understood when viewed within the context of industrial group relationships which are themselves rooted in history dating back to the early Tokugawa period of seventeenth-century Japan. These practices are based upon complex sets of relationships endogenous to Japanese society, which underlie a system of barriers and gates usually invisible to the uninitiated.

We conclude that the agency theorists' view of the Japanese main bank relationship has been predicated upon a selection bias in data which has led to a number of mistaken assumptions, first, relating to the interpretation of governance functions, in particular to bank monitoring and cross-shareholding, and, second, totally overlooking the fact that for the main bank, the relationship itself is the bank's greatest source of profits. Although the agency approach is itself grounded in the concept of a set of marketable contractual rights embodied in the Anglo-Dutch concept of the joint-stock company, to which the theory appears to be culturally bound, the theory purports to be a universalistic one. By refusing to account for, or even allow for cultural variables, however, agency theorists have blinded themselves to the consideration of any alternative hypotheses. Our analysis is the antithesis of those propounded by such market-based theories; instead, we propose an alternative, communal framework within which the two Japanese governance structures, the *kigyo shudan* and *keiretsu*, are placed.

Furthermore, we conclude that the very essence of Japanese governance structures is not always predominantly synergistic, as the *kigyo shudan* form tends to be, but, as evidenced by the *keiretsu* form, is often rooted in the exploitation of asymmetries of information, labor, and a host of other variables in the sets of relationships that permeate Japanese society. Our holistic model, the Relational Access Paradigm, provides a framework to better understand the dimensions of power, information, and access that define Japanese governance structures.

2 Developing Theory from Practice: A Methodological Approach

LAYING THE GROUNDWORK FOR THE RESEARCH

When I began my fieldwork in Japan in June–July 1992, it was not a country with which I was unfamiliar. I had studied the Japanese language as an university undergraduate in the mid-1960s and had lived in Japan in 1971–72 as a graduate student. Since then Japan has been a country in which I have been immersed both professionally, for business and research, and personally, having made numerous trips over the years as well to visit family and friends. Tokyo has been a second home, a city whose many changes I had chronicled for the past twenty-five years and whose labyrinthine personality was almost as familiar to me as my native New York. Although Japan itself has changed over the past quarter century and become much more cosmopolitan, in many ways the fundamental patterns of traditional relationships remain unaltered, especially the subtle etiquette of interpersonal relations governing all of business life, which we discuss further in Chapters 3 and 4. As I embarked on this research project, I was well aware of the pitfalls and accustomed to the daunting limitations which all too often beset researchers in Japan.

From the start I recognized that any methodological approach employed for the research would be in some senses like conducting business in Japan and would entail building long-term relationships. I knew that in a culture like Japan's, where information is highly uncodified, rigid differentiations are made between insiders and outsiders. Adherence to these distinctions permits the free flow of information among insiders. Japanese are accustomed to using such

11

terms as *yoso no hito*, someone from a different place—a stranger, when discussing someone who is not of their group or firm. Although Japanese researchers often express envy of the foreign researcher's access to Japanese corporate executives (a favor they are routinely denied), such access is in some senses a mere foot in the door. As a foreigner, one is the quintessential outsider, a *gaijin*—an alien (a term which could be applied equally well to an extraterrestrial). It is necessary to create relationships of trust with people in order to overcome barriers built to preserve the company's image. Hit-and-run surveys or single-shot interviews too often elicit only stock answers. (Just as we found that relational access had a significant bearing in enabling our research, Chapter 3 will discuss in some detail the implications of relational access, not as a methodological necessity, but as a theoretical concept.)

It was against this background that I first began the research for this book with a preliminary stay in Tokyo in June and July of 1992. During this time I met with some of my pre-existing contacts in both banking and academic circles to apprise them of my research plans and objectives, a prerequisite for smooth cooperation rather than a simple courtesy. I also conducted a limited preliminary round of interviews in order to begin to fine-tune the set of questions in my *aide mémoire*. I needed to determine not only whether I was asking the right questions but also whether my research objectives were within the realm of possibility. Banking is a profession which even in the West is well known for its reticence. In a culture such as Japan's, it was to be expected that there would be a great deal of non-codified, that is, unpublished, information which would be difficult, perhaps impossible, to come by.

Nevertheless, thanks to personal contacts that I had developed in the Japanese banking industry during my years as publisher and editor-in-chief of *Japan Financial Market Report*, and subsequently in my position as Senior Research Fellow at the Kinyu Zaisei Jijo Kenkyu-kai (Institute for Financial Affairs), I was fortunate that my contacts were able to arrange personal introductions to personnel in key areas within the banking industry. Given the generally closed nature of Japanese society to outsiders and the deliberately opaque character of their financial institutions in particular, my contacts proved to be an invaluable resource in supplying the level and the quality of cooperation I received from the interview respondents.

TESTING AND DEVELOPING THEORY:
THE CASE STUDY METHOD

The research began with a clearly described and limited objective: to investigate and describe how the monitoring operations of the Japanese main bank system were conducted by its bank team. Some agency theory economists (see Chapter 5) have proposed the main bank as corporate governor and monitoring agent, not only on behalf of other creditors, but also for other shareholders in the client firm. One generally cited proof of this was the existence of the bank teams whose purported function was to report on the financial well-being of the firms to which they were assigned. The hypothesized role of the bank team was only a single sub-hypothesis in a more encompassing theory regarding the Japanese main bank system which viewed the Japanese main bank as essentially an agent of multiple interests, including other firms in its group, other banks, and indirectly government economic policy. It was the initial focus of our research to gather the evidentiary data on what the main bank teams were intended for and what they actually did.

The study commenced with an initial definition of the research question: to investigate how the monitoring operations of the Japanese main bank system were conducted by its bank team [Mintzberg, 1979]. By focusing on monitoring within the broader context of the main bank relationship, it was expected that the study would be able to pinpoint the data to be systematically gathered. Later, our findings would switch the focus of the research from theory-testing research to theory-building. At this stage, however, after formulation of the research problem, the potentially important variables were defined principally in terms of the agency theory framework.

The overarching objective of the study was to collect empirical evidence against which agency and other theories could be tested. The research methodology centered on the fundamental premise that the development of testable, relevant, and valid theory should be grounded in intimate connections with empirical reality [Glaser and Strauss in *The Discovery of Grounded Theory,* 1967; and Eisenhardt in "Building Theories from Case Study Research," 1989]. The case study approach was chosen as the most appropriate methodology because it not only allows for the continuous comparison of data and theory but emphasizes both the emergence of theoretical categories during the process of data collection and an incremental approach to case selection and data gathering [Eisenhardt, 1989].

Over the course of the fieldwork, the use of the case study approach combined different data collection methods, including interviews, questionnaires (of other research teams), and the use of archival resources. The evidence gathered was both qualitative (verbal, anecdotal) and quantitative (numerical). Qualitative data was correlated with quantitative data from questionnaires and surveys [Yin, 1984].

Building the Pool of Interview Respondents

At the outset of the interview process, confidentiality was assured to each respondent as to his or her identity and the name of his or her institution. In addition, years of research experience in Japan had taught me not to adopt an overhasty attitude, particularly in the early interview stages, and to allow sufficient time for the interviewer–respondent relationship to develop before proceeding to the next round. As is true everywhere, but particularly in Japan, the proper points of the business culture and etiquette had to be followed to allow the right conditions to develop.

The use of the interview was the main research device in the study. Following the Grounded Theory approach [Glaser and Strauss, 1967], a focused semi-structured open-ended question technique in face-to-face interviews [Merton, Fiske, and Kendall, 1956] was employed with the Japanese practitioner respondents. This allowed me the flexibility to pursue issues raised by responses which had not been anticipated from prior review of the existing literature on the main bank relationship. An *aide mémoire* was utilized, but at times it became necessary to probe by employing hypothetical scenarios to clarify questions or challenge pat responses.

The initial set of interviews in June and July 1992 went better than expected, especially considering their limited but crucial objective in setting a full agenda for my return that October and November. Even more important, my preliminary interviews with the bankers also began to raise some serious questions about the accuracy of the main bank hypothesis prevailing in Western academic circles. When I returned to Japan that fall, my banking industry contacts had arranged personal introductions for me in the appropriate departments of the leading banks, government ministries, and bankers associations. The focus of these first two rounds of interviews with bank practitioners were on the operations of the main bank relationship, specifically, the nature of the bank team and its responsibilities in the day-to-day handling of clients' affairs.

The process of information gathering was further aided by the extensive informal networks that exist in Japanese banks (and within Japanese society as a whole; see Chapter 3's discussion on high-context cultures and the diffusion of uncodified information). These networks are maintained by such mechanisms as employee *doki-kai* (informal "class" groups to which employees who have entered the firm in the same year belong), the normally frequent rotation of job assignments within the bank, temporary work assignments, as well as the frequent informational meetings that are held by work groups at all levels within the bank, within the banking industry, and lastly, but not least, by the monthly meetings of the retired directors of the bank—the *OB*s ("Old Boys").

Thus the "snowball sampling" method (referred introductions) [Bailey, 1978] was significantly enhanced by how well it fit in with the Japanese system of informal social/business networks and was very successfully employed in widening the pool of respondents. In each case, after receiving an introduction to the respondent, I would conduct the first interview and apprise them of my future research plans. I then allowed a suitable period of time to pass before requesting a follow-up interview. Between research stays in Japan I remained in touch with the informants through correspondence, letting them know of their valuable contribution to the progress of the research and seeking their assistance in providing introductions to particular categories of interview subjects needed to further the study.

The size of the respondent pool "snowballed" from the initial 13 respondents (June–July 1992), to 26 respondents (October–November 1992), 37 respondents (April 1993), 62 respondents (January–February 1994), and the last round, 71 respondents (November–December 1995). These interviews in Japan were supplemented with interviews with some of the respondents on their visits to New York.

The snowballing of referrals through successive rounds of interviews added the burden of many more weeks to each succeeding field trip to Japan. In order to maintain these relationships it was necessary to try and schedule an interview with each respondent on my every visit to Japan. Although the respondent pool grew rather large, there was also a natural attrition in its active members, some seventeen (24%) of the respondents had been transferred from the Tokyo metropolitan area, either to other regions of Japan (10), or overseas (7) through the normal rotation of job assignments, which typically occur every two or three years within Japanese banks. In fact, only two of the banking respondents remained in the same department (both were in their banks' research divisions); all the others had changed their positions at least once, or even twice during the four-year period.

The respondents can be divided into four categories based upon seniority and the authority indicated by title, a hierarchical distinction to which Japanese pay extreme attention in all situations, in business and otherwise. (See Table 2.1: Ranks of respondents.)

Table 2.1   Ranks of respondents

Rank *(Japanese title in parenthesis):*	Number	% by category
I Senior Management: Director *(Torishimari-yaku)* and above, including former directors and OBs	8	11.3%
II Middle Management: General Manager of Branch or Department, Deputy Gen. Manager *(Shiten-cho, Bu-cho, Ji-cho)*	*23*	*32.4%*
III Junior Management: Manager of Division, Section Chief *(Ka-cho, Chosai-yaku, Shunin)*	32	45.0%
IV Associates—lower ranking officers	8	11.3%

As is evident from the table, an effort was made to get a representative cross-sampling of respondents not only by category or type of institution but also by level of responsibility and position, which in Japanese hierarchical structure is closely correlated to age. One senior banker commented after reading an earlier draft of my research that "it was good that you interviewed bankers of all ages when you did your research." When I pointed out to him that the quotations in my paper did not identify the respondents by their ages or seniority, he further responded that their viewpoints, characteristically, often indicated their relative age category. Indeed, within the bank and the banking community, the most frank and self-critical comments of the industry came from the mid- to younger age members, those under forty years of age, while the more culture-bound comments came, predictably, from the more senior level personnel over the age of fifty-five. Senior bankers are well aware of the viewpoints of their more junior colleagues through the informal information structure they employ to sound them out, called *da-shin,* "listening to the reverberations" from ideas informally circulated by senior management among the junior employees.

Most of the respondents were interviewed a number of times over the full three-and-a-half-year course of the field research. This allowed relationships to move beyond the *tatemae* (outer façade) level of socially expected responses to the *honne* (real story) and frank interchanges. Wherever possible I attempted to cross-validate information given by a respondent by interviewing more than one respondent at that institution, thus obtaining multiple perspectives on the same set of questions. In several instances I was successful in finding a number of former employees of particular institutions and in those cases was able to further minimize the number of socially desired/expected or *tatemae* responses.

It is not that *tatemae* is not useful in its own right in reflecting the image that the respondent's company or group would like to promote. As the "official" company line, it is to be expected in initial interviews, particularly with the more senior executives. That kind of socially correct response, however, generally has little correspondence to reality and it is only when the *tatemae* façade has been dropped that some insight can be gained into actual banking business practices.

Selecting Subjects for Case Study

A variety of categories of banks was selected so that the main bank paradigm could be compared not only with the top-six city banks (major commercial banks) but also with the operations of long-term credit banks and the non-top-six city banks, trust, regional, and second-tier regional banks. Within these institutions various managerial levels and departments were then selected. The respondents were chosen, first, with the intent of substantiating previously reported findings and, later, to extend the evidentiary basis for other emergent hypotheses.

During the course of our research interviews were conducted with seventy-one Japanese respondents who consisted of executives at seven city banks, including the top six (*kigyo shudan*-affiliated) banks and a former specialized bank; two of the three long-term credit banks; three regional banks; two trust banks; one foreign-owned bank; and a government-owned bank. In addition, interviews were conducted with officials from the Ministry of Finance (MoF), Ministry of International Trade and Industry (MITI), the Postal Savings Bureau of the Ministry of Posts and Telecommunications, and six other regulatory and bank service organizations. (See Table 2.2: Summary of interview respondents.) These interviews were conducted during a four-year period between 1992 and 1995, in addition to the numerous but less formal interchanges with additional respondents in the course of the author's professional activities as Senior Research Fellow at the Kinyu Zaisei Jijo Kenkyu-kai (Institute for Financial Affairs).

A great amount of data was needed in order to get as complete a portrait as possible, since there was very little literature as to how the main bank relationship with its clients was actually managed. The highly stylized economic models were of little help. Altogether I conducted a total of 192 formal interviews (251.25 hours) with 71 respondents, each interview totaling 1 hour 18 minutes, on average. Among the major institutions included in the study (city and long-term credit banks), 106 interviews were conducted with the 38 respondents in these major banks. Although the number of cases and respondents was rather high, only after amassing a critical amount of data was I able to draw the theory-building connections needed to construct the paradigm.

Table 2.2   Summary of interview respondents

Bank	Number of respondents	Rank of respondents*	Number of interviews	Total hours
Top six city banks				
Bank "A"	6	1-II, 3-III, 2-IV	14	20h45m
Bank "B"	5	1-I; 2-II; 2-III	15	17h30m
Bank "C"	1	1-III	4	7h30m
Bank "D"	6	2-I; 1-II; 1-III; 2-IV	15	25 hrs
Bank "E"	2	2-III	5	4h30m
Bank "F"	1	1-III	3	4h10m
Other city banks				
Bank "G"	5	2-I; 2-II; 1-IV	17	20h35m
Long-term credit banks				
Bank "H"	9	2-II; 6-III; 1-IV	22	24h50m
Bank "I"	3	1-II; 2-III	11	16h25m
Regional banks				
Bank "J"	1	1-II	1	1h30m
Bank "K"	2	1-II; 1-IV	2	1h45m
Bank "L"	1	1-III	1	1hr
Trust banks				
Bank "M"	1	1-III	5	7h15m
Bank "N"	1	1-III	2	3h15m
Other banks				
Bank "O"	8	4-II; 4-III	25	35 hrs
Foreign owned bank				
Bank "P"	2	1-II; 1-IV	6	9h35m
Overseas bank of securities firm				
Bank "Q"	1	1-III	1	1hr
Relevant government ministries				
Ministry #1	1	1-III	3	2h30m
Ministry #2	2	2-II	2	2h30m
Ministry #3	2	2-III	3	3hrs
Banking associations and institutions				
Institution #1	2	1-II; 1-III	6	6hrs
Institution #2	1	1-I	1	1h30m
Institution #3	4	1-I; 1-II; 2-III	8	19 hrs
Institution #4	1	1-II	1	1h30m
Consulting firms to financial services industry				
Firm #1	1	1-I	7	10 hrs
Firm #2	1	2-II	1	3h30m

* Rank of respondents corresponds to Table 2.1.

FROM THEORY TESTING TO THEORY BUILDING: CRAFTING INSTRUMENTS AND PROTOCOLS

As the research progressed and the objective shifted from hypothesis-testing to theory-building, correlations began to appear between quantitative research findings and the qualitative evidence [Yin, 1984]. Quantitative statistical data collected by larger-scale Japanese research teams to which we had access affected the overall research pattern, first, by suggesting that some hypotheses were more probable than others, and secondly, by providing strong substantiation for our emerging theory of relational access, described in Chapter 3. For example, quantitative data added concrete insight as to where the main bank stood in the *uchi–soto* (insider–outsider) continuum of relationships (Chapter 7). Among other things, it helped define how the view of the main bank relationship differed across large firms and small firms. Statistical data also revealed in quantifiable terms how the relationship was paid for, raising serious questions as to the accuracy of some of the prevailing hypotheses.

The process followed by the research reflected the synergistic relationship described by Mintzberg [1979]:

> For while systematic data create the foundation for our theories, it is the anecdotal data that enable us to do the building. Theory building seems to require rich description, the richness that comes from anecdote. We uncover all kinds of relationships in our hard data, but it is only through the use of this soft data that we are able to explain them. [p. 587]

Nevertheless, despite the many hours I spent with Japanese researchers and subsequently analyzing the data, by and large I operated as a single researcher, conducting interviews with a tape recorder as the second listener. Typically I was only able to get to making the transcriptions of the tapes many weeks after the interviews due to the hectic pace of my days and nights in Japan which were crammed with innumerable meetings and after-hours get-togethers with an ever-widening circle of practitioner respondents. Within this context my tape recorder acquired the character of a second researcher, faithfully recording at all times, including the less inhibited thoughts and feelings of respondents during relaxed conversations in the evening. While most interviews were usually held in a conference room at the respondent's bank, at other times they were held in restaurants, coffee lounges, and other less formal settings. Note taking under such circumstances was more difficult. By far the most revealing and least inhibited interviews took place after work hours in pubs. Needless to say the conviviality of the atmosphere, further aided by beer and *sake*, left the respondent, if not the interviewer, more voluble, and, in those cases, the practice of recording and subsequent transcription often revealed the frankest and most startling *honne*.

The later rehearing of the tape and readings of the transcriptions often presented new and sometimes different perspectives than the ones I had been able to make note of at the time, giving me a fresh viewpoint to reflect upon, once outside of the fray. The tape recorder thus played the role of a resident devil's advocate [Eisenhardt, 1989], pointing up seemingly contradictory responses from different respondents as well as other anomalies that would require further clarification. As I drew up the next set of questions for another round of interviews, I made a point of taking full advantage of these contradictions, using them to elicit fuller and deeper explanations.

Clearly, this approach involved the frequent overlap of data analysis with data collection during the research. Eisenhardt provided justification for such overlap by distinguishing data collection methods in theory-building research from theory-testing research [1989]. In theory-building case research, she argued, the researcher's objective is to understand each case individually and in depth, not to create a uniformly obtained set of statistical data about a set of observations (such as from a questionnaire). When new insights emerge during the research, it makes sense to alter the data collection tools to allow the study to probe such themes or to take advantage of special opportunities in a given situation.

The interview protocol used in my research was an *aide mémoire* that formed the core of the interview process. It was important, however, to be able to add to the protocol as the study progressed in order to respond to the theory-building goals of the research. However, I regarded such flexibility, not as a license to be unsystematic, but rather only permitting the study to pursue the uniqueness of a specific case, in Eisenhardt's words, a "controlled opportunism."

ANALYZING THE DATA AND SHAPING
THE HYPOTHESIS

Within-case data was collected principally by multiple interviews at each institution across multiple levels of informants and served two fundamental purposes: cross-substantiation of the data provided by individual respondents, and different perspectives and observations within the same institution of the same organizational processes. The objective was not so much to create rich portraits of individual institutions as to be able to generalize patterns across cases. Therefore, for example, different types of banks were selected to compare management issues and strategies. These cases were then sifted into various categories including corporate group *(kigyo shudan)* membership and status, large versus small size bank/firm, historicity of firm/bank relationship. Some of these variables revealed very little, but other relationships such as historicity, size, and above all the firm's financial performance and dependency on bank financing led to important patterns of inter- and intra-group dimensions, suggesting new and unanticipated categories, connections, and concepts.

Constructing a Hypothesis: A Reiterative Process

As one set of qualitative data was reinforced by the next set of data, ongoing comparisons between interview responses and theory began to illumine an apparently deep rift between prevailing theory and actual practice and to suggest that some different hypotheses were necessary. The first step, we found, required a redefinition of some basic terminology and concepts. For example, the common usage of the term "keiretsu" obscured, if not obliterated, the fundamental structural differences among Japanese industrial groups. As another example, the term "main bank," while inviting comparison with the German *Hausbank,* was, in fact, quite different than its would-be German counterpart, the Japanese "main bank" being a contradiction in terms since a large firm could have several "main" banks, all competing for its business. We found that such misreadings of these terms (and others) served to further promulgate misconceptions about the character and relationships of firms and groups within the Japanese milieu. Repeated encounters with respondents indicated that these differences of terminology were not merely semantic quibbles over nomenclature but implied larger theoretical misconstructions of the Japanese business environment.

It was thus necessary to use more precise definitions and propose alternative constructs which were based on the ongoing process of analyzing the accumulating data. Such hypotheses, definitions, and the measurement of the evidence emerged from an iterative procedure of collecting and analyzing data, rather than from *a priori* constructs. Central to that process was the use of multiple sources of evidence, both qualitative and quantitative, as earlier described.

Testing the hypotheses with the evidence in each case was essential. In this regard the qualitative data supplied by interview informants provided crucial insight and support towards establishing the validity of the hypotheses. Through interviewing, the possible rationales underlying the relationships that the data seem to suggest could be probed. As Eisenhardt [1989] wrote:

> Qualitative data often provides a good understanding of the dynamic underlying the relationship, that is, the "why" of what is happening. . . . Just as in hypothesis-testing research an apparent relationship may simply be a spurious correlation or may reflect the impact of some third variable on each of the other two. Therefore it is important to discover the underlying theoretical reasons for why the relationship exists. This helps to establish the internal validity of the findings. [p. 542]

In sum, unlike the use of questionnaires, through the reiterative process of repeat interviews it was possible to cover the same basic questions with all of the respondents on the first round and then to follow up on and explore anomalies in the responses during succeeding rounds of interviews. This provided the flexibility to test and build constructs and the ability to search more deeply into underlying issues so as to modify those constructs.

Triangulation of Data

The triangulation of qualitative data with the quantitative data [Jick, 1979] of two other research teams [Omura, 1993, and Fuji

Sogo Kenkyujo, 1993] resulted in a highly synergistic combination that further strengthened our study. The quantitative data produced by these two other studies was compiled from the written responses to questionnaires sent to firm executives as to their firm's relative relationship with its banks and with its other cross-shareholding partners. I also spent some ten hours with the chief researcher of the Fuji Sogo Kenkyujo report, and two hours with Professor Kei'ichi Omura discussing the details of our respective data and the closeness of the data fit and my conclusions. Triangulation was not only achieved on a qualitative–quantitative basis, but also along bank-versus-firm vectors, which presented remarkably close mirror images of each other.

The different types of data collection methods, interviews versus questionnaires, one qualitative, the other quantitative, exploit the unique insights possible from the different methods of data collection. When a pattern is corroborated by the evidence from another set of data, the finding is stronger and better grounded. The use of differently structured and diverse methods improves the likelihood of accurate and reliable theory, that is, a theory with a close fit with the data [Eisenhardt, 1989].

SITUATING THEORY WITHIN THE LITERATURE

As the study progressed towards developing its own theoretical perspective, it was also essential for that viewpoint to be situated within the extant literature. The literature which presented findings similar to our own, however, tied together underlying similarities in phenomena not normally associated in the literatures of either economics or management. Thus, in Chapter 3, in reviewing economic theories of the firm, the discussion first contrasts the Western economic model with theories of what we term the communal forms, as exemplified in the fief and clan forms. The discussion then broadens these communal forms beyond the firm to include the two forms of Japanese industrial groups, the *keiretsu* and the *kigyo shudan*. Our paradigm then seeks to extend these models beyond their uni-dimensional definitions to add a dimension heretofore not considered in pre-existing theories of the firm. This new framework is termed the Relational Access Paradigm. In Chapter 4, the literatures of anthropology and sociology are employed to expand upon the embeddedness of the cultural and historical background of economic relations as it relates to the concepts of household and the foundations of the Japanese firm and their industrial groups, which is again reinforced by the Relational Access Paradigm.

Key to the comparison of emergent theory with extant literature is to encompass a broad range of literature, including literature which conflicts with the theory, such as the work of the theorists and researchers discussed in Chapter 5. There the work of several researchers are examined whose theories evolved beyond Nakatani's basic proposition of risk-sharing among *kigyo shudan* firms and the centrality of the group's bank in that process, to the agency approach of main bank monitoring and governance construct of Aoki, Hoshi, and Sheard. The contributions of Miwa and Horiuchi *et al.*, who had raised some serious doubts which were never responded to by Nakatani, Aoki, Hoshi, or Sheard, are also reviewed.

The field-testing of these various conflicting hypotheses was an integral aspect of the research process which allowed the study to move beyond existing contradictory hypotheses to begin to formulate and then to apply its own theoretical concept of relational access to the main bank's relationship with its client firm. The juxtaposition of conflicting results acted as a motive force to drive the research into more creative, frame-breaking modes of thought to deeper insights into both the emergent theory and the extant literature [Eisenhardt, 1989]. Although the grounded theory case-study method is rarely used in finance, my experience suggests that it can be a highly useful methodology.

REACHING CLOSURE:
A THEORETICAL SATURATION POINT

Two-and-a-half years into my fieldwork, I had felt that I had reached a theoretical saturation point [Glaser and Strauss, 1967]. At that point, with a base of sixty-two respondents, additional incremental learning became more limited as the observation of new phenomena with each new respondent became minimal. In January and February 1994 I circulated a draft report [Scher, 1993] of my interview data among the respondents for their reaction. Some thirty-eight practitioner respondents reviewed this preliminary report and gave me their reactions.

While all of the respondents noted the report's accuracy in rendering their own views, their comments on the report as a whole characteristically reflected their positions (and ages). The more senior and some mid-level respondents seemed a bit discomfited by the frankness with which the bank's motivations in its client relationships were portrayed. More junior-level respondents commended the report for exposing the anachronisms of a system which they felt needed change. The most senior respondents, the *OB*s, retired from the fray, complimented the report's capturing a long-view perspective and rich detail of the subject. In Chapter 6 we will examine in some detail their portrayal of the main bank relationship.

My Relational Access Paradigm and its development (presented in Chapter 3) was measurable because it was generated and verified during the theory building process, and, because it was so intimately tied to the evidence, it was therefore empirically valid. The constant juxtaposition of the conflicting data with established theoretical positions opened a new path that broke with typical theory building based on incremental studies or armchair axiomatic deduction.

3 Relational Access versus the Western Economic Paradigm

In this chapter we set forth the theoretical groundwork for the major premises presented here. First, we argue that prevailing Western economic theories of the firm have historically engaged too narrow a paradigm by overgeneralizing certain basic assumptions and by limiting their conceptual framework to a nonorganic view of the firm. We survey those theories in turn, annotating the criticisms and focusing on the two leading theories: agency theory, which typically sees the firm as a nexus of contracts, and the transaction-cost economics theory, which takes a market-versus-hierarchy approach. Second, we incorporate the existing theories of clan and fief forms of the firm into our discussion, examining the limited perspective of these analyses, and how they differ from the previously examined models. Finally, we reshape the clan and fief modes within a generalized communal form to create a new holistic paradigm of the firm. We create this synthesis by adding a dimensionality absent from the market-bureaucracy continuum and the nexus of contracts linear paradigms. This third dimension, a relational access continuum of insider–outsider relationships, leads to a more holistic paradigm that reveals hitherto unexplored governance structures and which more accurately explains the inter- and intrafirm characteristics typical of Japanese industrial groups and their member firms.

ECONOMIC THEORIES OF THE FIRM

From Production Plans to Transaction Efficiencies: The Development of Theory

All of the major economic theories of the firm—Neoclassical, Principal–Agent, Nexus of Contracts, Commodity/Property Rights,

27

and Transaction Cost—tend to view the firm within four basic definitions: (1) as a legal entity; (2) as an administrative entity; (3) as a pool of physical facilities, learned skills, and liquid capital; and (4) in a capitalist economy, as the primary instrument for the production of goods and services and for the planning and allocation of future production and distribution. Neoclassical Theory, perhaps the most rudimentary analysis of the modern firm, views the firm as essentially a set of production plans in which the manager supervises production to maximize the owner's welfare, i.e., the present value of the firm and/or profits. It is assumed that the owner has two primary rights and responsibilities: to select the production program and to appropriate the residual [Hart, 1989].

Building on the basic dichotomy between manager and owner, Principal–Agent Theory, or agency theory, perceives a fundamental conflict of interest between ownership and professional management. Although still adhering to the concept of a set of production plans, agency theory posits that managers may at times advance their objectives at the expense of the owners/shareholders, thus laying the basis for the beginnings of a managerial theory of the firm. An essential predicate of agency theory, like much of Western management theory, is that human motivation is universal and, in the organizational sphere, driven principally by the economic incentives of wages and personal gain. We discuss later on how this view, by overextending its reach to non-Western cultures, i.e., Japan, has led some theorists to misread the purposes and functions of some of the informal elements of the organization of Japanese industrial groups. Agency theory has evolved to become one of the two major accepted descriptions of the workings of management capitalism [Berle and Means, 1932] (along with transaction-cost theory).

Western economic theories of the firm today generally center on the powers necessary for control. Such theories tend to view major issues within the framework of the principal–agent relationship— from the loss of control by owners due to the dispersion of ownership in publicly traded companies, to highly sophisticated considerations of governance within a polity organized through a division of labor and rewards. Some agency theories emphasize defining the firm as an entity. On the other hand, the nexus of contracts view, advanced by agency theorists Jensen and Meckling [1976], describes the firm as simply a bundle of contracts, contractual relations with employees, customers, creditors, or suppliers, whether these contracts are internal or external to the firm, and whatever the form of the firm—public corporation, closely-held firm, or partnership. Later, in Chapter 5, we discuss the agency approach as its proponents attempt to apply it to governance in Japan.

The issue of corporate form raises legal and administrative questions relating to the transferability of property rights, leading some theorists to conclude that how property rights are defined in turn defines the nature of the firm. The approach which views the firm as a set of property rights, first proposed by Demsetz [1967], and later expanded upon by others, identifies a firm with all the nonhuman assets that belong to it, including machinery, buildings and locations, cash, client lists, patents and copyrights, and the rights and obligations of outstanding contracts that are transferable. The firm is the assets which the firm owners possess by virtue of being owners, together with the residual rights of control over those assets which can be used in any way consistent with custom, law, or prior contract.

Commodity Theory sharpens the distinctions drawn by the nexus of contracts theory, but leaves the questions of ownership raised by property rights theorists largely untouched. Putterman [1988] advances commodity theory by pointing out that the firm which he defines as "a commodity—a bundle of rights with a marketable value linked to an expected profit stream," must be ownable and salable. Viewing the firm as a commodity, however, does not take into account its human assets, since management and workers cannot be bought and sold. Putterman offers two conceptualizations here. One theory views human assets as a production coalition or team of stakeholders which includes some or all of the following players: equity owners, debt holders, members of the board of directors, managers, production workers, materials suppliers, and customers. Each of the parties can be viewed as competing in a noncooperative game with an incentive to free-ride on the joint value-maximizing contributions of the other parties.

The second view regards the same group of parties either as an association, with a formal decision-making structure, or as a polity resembling a coalition. Distributive issues are settled largely within the sphere of exchange among a broad set of interacting agents. It is

Putterman's conclusion that even if workers held an ownership stake in the firm they would still prefer to rent their services in exchange for contractual wages, because their very freedom to sell or withdraw their services provides them a unique advantage over the other shareholders. In societies that lack free labor markets, however, the inference that to de-commoditize labor would also de-commoditize the firm and, by extension, the property rights system itself has important implications to our later discussion of other captive-market relationships in communal-firm models, such as with subcontractors, vendors, and even customers.

Transaction cost economics theory, introduced by Ronald Coase [1937], traces the existence of the firm to the thinking, planning, and transaction costs usually ignored in the neoclassical model. Coase's theory sees the firm as a hierarchy of decision-making which effectively suppresses marketplace negotiation in the allocation of resources within the firm, with consequential losses in learning through the interactions normally associated with the marketplace. It is this power of decision-making authority that he uses to define the firm. The approaches known as transaction cost theories emphasize the efficiency (cost savings) of such organizational arrangements.

In his 1937 article "The Nature of the Firm," Coase stated: "Outside the firm, price movements direct production. Market prices are discovered in the interaction of available supplies and effective demand. Within the firm, these market transactions are eliminated. In place of the complicated market structure with exchange transaction is substituted the entrepreneur-coordinator, who directs production. . . . The distinguishing mark of the firm is the suppression of the price mechanism." One party, the entrepreneur-coordinator, in the absence of a market, is given authority to set the price of a commodity. This concentration of authority is what defines the firm. The efficiencies that ensue from reducing or eliminating haggling in the market set the boundaries of the firm in transactional terms.

Williamson [1975] further elaborated transaction cost economics by opposing two distinct idealized modes—the market mode versus the hierarchical mode. The market transactional form consists of specified contractual relationships, both long-term and spot transactions, and is the most efficient form when there is little ambiguity over performance. He argues, however, for the efficiency of the second mode, the hierarchical-bureaucratic form, where transactions rely upon explicit rules and procedures, without any simple criteria for profit maximization or cost minimization. According to Williamson, the hierarchical authority generates fair and legitimate judgments in the long run.

Williamson [1985] suggests some limitations to the transaction cost model. Taking Coase's major idea of the firm's ability to economize on transaction costs, Williamson points out that once certain investment decisions are made, such as the location of a plant, the training of a workforce, the expansion of plant capacity to meet a particular customer's needs, or the relocation of a worker, to a large extent the parties are locked into the relationship and external market prices are no longer a guide to the parties' opportunity costs.

Transaction cost theory has been criticized by Alchian and Demsetz for its basic assumption that the employee will always act as required by the employer. In actual practice, they argue, authority relations too often fall short of the model. Alchian and Demsetz [1972] advance the idea that transactions involving joint or team production require monitoring of each participant's contribution so that it can be assessed. Those best placed to monitor these transactions are the owners of the firm, who are defined by the following characteristics: (1) status as a residual claimant; (2) an ability to observe input behavior; (3) status as a party to all contracts with inputs; (4) the power to change the management team; and (5) the power to sell these rights. They thus reiterate the dichotomy between owner and manager.

Although one approach to resolving the tensions of the owner/manager dichotomy may be to fix transaction costs through long-term pre-investment contracts, committing to terms of trade in every conceivable variable, the resulting negotiating and enforcement cost would be prohibitive. Still, in many ways, Western commercial contracts often attempt to accomplish such ends, and all too frequently end up in extensive, costly litigation [Williamson, 1985]. One alternative is for the parties to negotiate and renegotiate the many uncodified terms of the relationship as it proceeds.

Williamson looks to hierarchical control in the form of the integration of the firm as a solution to the ills of the marketplace, although it is not always most preferable to the market. Integration of the firm would bring all disputes out of the market (and the courts) and into the firm, where the power of executive authority would presumably settle any disputes by fiat. In such a highly integrated world there would be no need for the market, or for litigation. This position, however, does not explain how taking the transaction within the firm can prevent contractual failure, since the firm itself rests on key contractual relations, such as employment contracts.

In sum, although it was Coase's insight that the costs of exchange in the capitalist firm do matter, Williamson argues, first, that the natural tendency of firms is to reduce their transaction costs by suppressing market price mechanisms through their internalization of (imperfect) markets in the form of hierarchies and, second, that the boundaries of firms are located where the costs of hierarchy (organization, management costs) are as efficient as the cost of an extra transaction in the marketplace. However, in this market-versus-hierarchy theoretical debate, it can be argued that in the real world firms try to maximize profits by doing both—by reducing transaction costs *and* by increasing their power in the marketplace [Pitelis, 1995].

COMMUNAL FORMS

Ouchi [1980] significantly expands Williamson's [1975] dichotomy of the market form and the bureaucratic form into a trichotomy by adding a third category, the "clan form" to transaction cost theory's taxonomy of organizational forms. His usage of the term "clan" is derived from Durkheim's [1893/1933] usage, denoting an organic association which resembles a kin network but which does not necessarily include blood relations. The members of the clan transact on an informal basis of shared information, personal trust, and equality.

In its internal governance Ouchi's clan form is based upon an understanding held in common by all parties to a particular transaction that, while imbalances in individual inducements and contributions may exist in the short term, in the long run balance will be restored and maintained. A generalized norm of reciprocity [Gouldner, 1960] is part of the environment which will produce a state of "serial equity," as opposed to the "spot equity" characteristic of markets and, to some extent, of bureaucracies as well. It is also assumed that in certain transaction environments, where no explicit, pre-specified measures of inducements and contributions exist, the parties to the clan form of transaction will trust in the generalized norm of reciprocity that underlies the relationship.

The willingness to permit short-term imbalances with the expectation of long-run balance or serial equity is an important feature of clan forms. In its internal manifestation it can be connected to lifetime employment together with personnel evaluation policies that emphasize qualitative rather than a purely quantitative evaluation. For example, managers who sacrifice their quantitative performance in the short term for the overall good of the company know that they will be appropriately recognized and compensated in the long run [Ouchi, 1981; Barney and Ouchi, 1984]. In its external form, it is shown by the belief among transacting partners that short-term imbalances will be remembered and compensated.

Expanding the categories of the transactional forms described by Williamson, Ouchi and others, Boisot [1986], and later Boisot and Child [1988], added the "fief form." In a number of respects this form appears both to draw from Weber's [1921/1947] "patrimonial bureaucracy" as well as to encompass the governance characteristics of household-style firms, both of which we discuss in the next chapter. Boisot and Child also restructured the hierarchy versus market dichotomy into a four-quadrant matrix of ideal types: bureaucracies, markets, fiefs, and clans. They differentiated these four forms on the basis of information asymmetries across two intersecting axes, a continuum of undiffused to diffused information and a second continuum of uncodified to codified information. Through its focus on information, this schema also was able to encompass and categorize: the nature of personal relationships intrafirm, impersonal or personal, hierarchical or competitive; goal-setting within the firm, superordinate or individualistic; coordination within the firm, horizontal or hierarchical; and whether a cultural system of shared values and beliefs is necessary.

High Context–Low Context/Power Relations:
Toward a More Holistic Model

In our reinterpretation of the transactional model, the addition of the above attributes to the description of the firm effectively transforms the transaction cost perspective from a nonorganic into an organic approach in which the firm is viewed as an integral part of a broader context. Relationships and actions are no longer purely contractual and economic; rather, they have been broadened to include culturally-based governance structures. Furthermore, as used in our paradigm, this more culturally inclusive model is framed not only by an x-axis defined by the diffusion of information and bounded by the polarities of markets and hierarchies, but also by a new y-axis of codified to uncodified information of the Boisot–Child framework, which, we argue, is one of the key conditions differentiating the purely Western economic paradigm from communal models. (See Figure 3.1.)

We further reinterpret and modify Boisot and Child's construction, which describes *intra*firm transactions (they applied it to Chinese enterprises), to include *inter*firm relationships and apply this matrix to firm–industrial group relationships. We believe that the nature of Japanese interfirm relationships, specifically groups of enterprises that are only *informally* linked, has never fit the market-versus-hierarchy dichotomy which pointedly ignores the social embeddedness of economic relations and transactions [Granovetter, 1985]. Such analyses fail to account for relationships which are opaque to outsiders but which exert a commanding influence upon business groups, industries, and markets. When we extend the information codification/diffusion paradigm to our interfirm analogs, two of the outstanding characteristics of Japanese interfirm relations immediately stand out, namely, their common reliance on a superstructure of shared beliefs and their adherence to informal codes of behavior.

This analysis is aided by the work of social psychologists and anthropologists. Hall [1977] classified Japan as a "high-context culture," indicating a high degree of shared assumptions and outlook often taken for granted by members of the society, which is maintained by extensive networks, both formal and informal, for the

Figure 3.1 Information codification and diffusion, high–low context/power relations matrix

	Undiffused Information **Hierarchical Power Relations**	**Diffused Information** **Horizontal Power Relations**
Low Context **Codified Information**	**Bureaucracies** • Information diffusion limited and under central control • Relationships impersonal and hierarchical • Submission to superordinate goals • Hierarchical coordination • No necessity to share values and beliefs • Explicit internal contracts, monitoring	**Markets** • Information diffused, no control • Relationships impersonal and competitive • No superordinate goals—each one for himself • Horizontal coordination through self-regulation • No necessity to share values and beliefs • Explicit market contracts, monitoring
High Context **Uncodified Information**	**Fiefs (Patrimonial Bureaucracy)** **Keiretsu—(vertical)** **Asymmetrical Power Relationships** **Subsidiary-like Affiliations** • Information diffusion limited by lack of codification to face-to-face relationships • Relationships personal and hierarchical • Submiss on to superordinate goals • Hierarchical coordination • Necessity to share values and beliefs • Implicit "internal" contracts, self-monitoring	**Clans (Kinship Network)** **Kigyo Shudan—(horizontal)** **Collegial Relationships** **Non-Competitive Synergistic Alliances** • Information is diffused but still limited by lack of codification to face-to-face relationships • Relationships personal but nonhierarchical • Goals shared through process of negotiation • Horizontal coordination through negotiation • Necessity to share values and beliefs • Implicit relational contracts, non-monitoring

Source: Adapted from Boisot and Child [1988] and the concepts of Durkheim [1893/1933], Hall [1977], Hofstede [1991], Ouchi [1980], Weber [1921/1947], Williamson [1975].

diffusion of uncodified information.[1] Hofstede [1991] introduced the concept of "Power Distance" to examine relationships in which there were varying degrees of inequality in the concentration of authority. To incorporate Hall's and Hofstede's concepts, we further modify the matrix to include two key factors. In our model, Hall's concept of high-context, low-context culture is correlated to information diffusion and codification (high context/uncodified and low context/codified). We also modify the information diffusion axis, correlating it to Hofstede's concept of power distance relationships. This power relationship axis, when applied to our interfirm analogs, distinguishes the fief form (*keiretsu*) characterized by feudal/asymmetrical power relations, from the clan form (*kigyo shudan*) characterized by collegial/non-competitive synergistic relations. Figure 3.2 illustrates the power relationships inherent in the two differing forms, as well as the relationship between the two forms, in contrast to the uni-dimensional schema usually used to represent the interfirm relationships of the former *zaibatsu* groups (see Appendix for a typical example).

At the top of Figure 3.2 is the *zaibatsu* holding company, the apex of a pyramidal control structure. These holding companies, abolished after World War II, were owned by a *zaibatsu* family, whose origins and postwar dissolution will be discussed in much greater detail in Chapters 4 and 5. They held stock in the firms which today comprise the *kigyo shudan*'s group member firms and their affiliated *keiretsu* firms' members. Today's *kigyo shudan* comprise a group of firms which are no longer owned by a holding company but instead are *horizontally* linked together and usually centered around the group's bank and/or trading company. For example, such former *zaibatsu* groups as Mitsui, Sumitomo, and Mitsubishi now consist of a number of related firms operating on essentially equal footing. A single member firm of such a *kigyo shudan* may in turn head a *keiretsu* of vertically affiliated companies. The old *zaibatsu* holding company system comprised both the *kigyo shudan* and the *keiretsu* structures.

---

[1] "Culture," as used by anthropologists, is a technical term referring to a system for creating, sending, storing, and processing information developed by human beings. The terms *mores, tradition, custom*, and *habit* are subsumed under the umbrella of "culture" [Hall and Hall, 1990].

37

Figure 3.2 Kigyo shudan–keiretsu power relationships: a three dimensional view

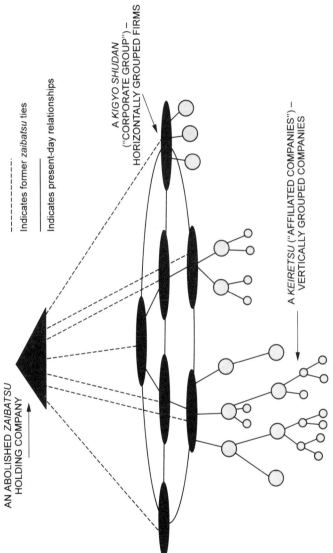

AN ABOLISHED ZAIBATSU
HOLDING COMPANY

Indicates former zaibatsu ties

Indicates present-day relationships

A KIGYO SHUDAN
("CORPORATE GROUP") –
HORIZONTALLY GROUPED FIRMS

A KEIRETSU ("AFFILIATED COMPANIES") –
VERTICALLY GROUPED COMPANIES

A *kigyo shudan* typically includes a cross-section of major indus-trial firms which are sometimes incorrectly referred to as "financial keiretsu" or "inter-market keiretsu."[2] They have been frequently confused with *keiretsu*, their *vertically* affiliated subordinate com-panies, which usually reflect multi-tiered supplier and distributor relationships. The distinction between the *kigyo shudan* and *keiretsu* is important because the nature of the power relationship is not the same; in the former there is a collegial relationship among the member companies whereas in the latter there is a hierarchy between the company and its affiliated subordinates.

The *kigyo shudan* form is typified by joint projects, usually between two principal industrial members of the group who are forming a subsidiary to develop and manufacture a new product or service. Generally, the group trading company serves a supporting role in project planning, development, and marketing, while among the group's financial institutions the main bank supplies financial expertise and long-term and short-term credit, and the group's trust bank may supply long-term project financing. Insurance companies, in addition to underwriting property and casualty insurance for the project, may also provide general financing, while other group companies provide project logistical support in areas such as ship-ping and transport, or technical expertise. However, each company's primary concern is with its own bottom line, so that depending upon the particular group, only some 20–30% of *kigyo shudan* company contracts these days are with other group members, compared to some 80% among the prewar *zaibatsu*.

The *keiretsu* form is exemplified by such well-known Japanese subcontracting practices as "Just In Time" manufacturing [Fruin, 1992], and black box design [Nishiguchi, 1992]. These practices, which shift inventory and product development costs to captive sets of subcontractors, are driven by a competitive dual-vendor pricing regime [Fruin, 1992] which pits at least two suppliers for each and

---

[2] Banks do have their own "keiretsu" relationships, but their vertical affiliations are with other financial institutions such as: regional banks, mutual banks, finance companies, casualty insurers, leasing companies and other financial services. Fifteen out of the top sixteen companies in which city, regional and long-term credit banks held shares were in fact other financial institutions [Zenkoku Shoken Torihikijo Kyogikai, 1992].

every component against each other. Suppliers are expected to absorb any increases in the cost of production. What may be long-term relationships within the *keiretsu* are dictated by short-term contracts that often require price reductions upon contract renewal [Sako, 1992].

Some theorists have attempted to describe attributes of Japanese industrial groups to fit a market or bureaucracy profile. For example, agency economists have viewed the diffusion of information among Japanese firms in both the vertical hierarchy (*keiretsu*) and in the horizontal/collegial mode (*kigyo shudan*) as part of an agency relationship. In our view, the evidence (presented in later chapters) tends to contradict such single-sided interpretation. Rather, in a high-context setting characterized by face-to-face relations, unlike either the bureaucracy or market forms, we have found that information diffusion tends to be personal, constant, wide-ranging, and generally unfocused.

Our model brings together some of the outstanding shared attributes of the *keiretsu* (fief) and *kigyo shudan* (clan) forms, including informal communication among firms of the group, chiefly through personal contact and membership in a culture of common values, while at the same time our model underscores the key distinctions between the fief form's essentially vertical mode, characterized by hierarchical relations in which control often masquerades as negotiations, and the clan form's essentially horizontal mode, which operates through collegial negotiation between related parties. Most importantly, however, our model emphasizes an issue unaccounted for in other models—the significance of the defining relationship, which we will now address.

THE RELATIONAL ACCESS PARADIGM: THE THIRD DIMENSION

The etymological origins of the Japanese word for relationship, "*kankei*," are derived from "*kan*" meaning a barrier-gate and "*kei*" signifying duty to the system. (The familial system will be discussed in some detail in Chapter 4.) These two elements capture and express the interplay of the basic concepts contained within the meaning of "relationship," namely, that access is determined by the nature of the relationship. "Access," first of all, as used in Japan, reflects a process not of opening doors but of controlling entry, determining who is allowed past the barrier-gate where passage is determined by the specifics of the relationship. For example, in the exclusionary Japanese business practice known as *dango* (collusive rigged bidding historically rooted in the guild system), access is afforded to a fixed group of contractors—to the exclusion of those considered outsiders, such as domestic newcomers and foreign bidders.

In current Japanese business parlance, a relationship may be "wet" (intimate, supportive) or "dry" (purely transactional) or non-existent (*"kankeinai"*) (no relationship and therefore no access at all). *Keiretsu torihiki,* group affiliated transactions, are mostly "dry," in contrast to transactions based, for example, on *giri,* in which obligational indebtedness makes the relationship very "wet." The nuanced and unstated (though understood) complexities of these relationships and the type of access each of them implies has led to the popularization by Japanese of the use of the English word "access," which skirts around the issues of implicit barriers and control. For example, for the past several years the official Japanese language texts of the Japan–U.S. trade negotiations has employed the English "access" written in *katakana* (Japanese phonetic alphabet) without definition. Such lack of information and explicit definition is to be expected in an uncodified/high context society.

This concept of implicit access and relationship is key to an understanding of the nature of Japanese industrial group relations, which has often been misconstrued by false assumptions of what constitutes the degree of "access."[3] In our discussion in future chapters the essence of these relationships will be of some importance in understanding the consequences of access for group members, shareholders, investors, other stakeholders, and for the main bank relationship in particular.

Normally the nature of transactions in the bureaucratic and the market forms are visible, with no opaque substructures to interfere

---

[3] Many Western scholars have come to mischaracterize Japanese long-term transactional relationships as dependent on "trust." This is not a concept or a word that is commonly used in Japan when describing *keiretsu torihiki* (group affiliated transactions). The right of "access" provided by a *keiretsu* relationship is seen as a franchise to do business that group membership affords, hence a "dry" relationship.

with the efficient use of the market or the rational conduct of the bureaucracy. By contrast, the fief and clan forms, that is, the *keiretsu* and the *kigyo shudan*, are characterized by an opacity based on relationships and customs, the implicit rules governing access to information and commerce. Such opacity is, as we discussed, relative and wholly dependent on one's relationships—as an outsider trying to deal with the system or as an insider who is part of the system.

It is our view that the implicit rules surrounding relational access operate as a basic principle which influences and often governs outcomes within intra- and intergroup relations. We call this principle the *uchi* (insider)–*soto* (outsider) continuum of graded relationships, ranging from "belonging" to "no relationship" and reflecting spheres of relationships that exist within sets and subsets.

As earlier discussed, the linear market dichotomy was reconceptualized by the inclusion of context (codification of information) into a more complex four-quadrant matrix (Figure 3.1). We have redrawn this matrix as a Cartesian plane (see Figure 3.3: The relational access paradigm: the third dimension), in which the x-axis represents power relationships (information diffusion), and the y-axis repres-ents high/low context (information codification). To this we have added a plane which intersects the matrix and is labeled the r-dimension, representing the *uchi–soto* continuum of relational access. In our model, the *uchi–soto* continuum is as basic a concept as those of power relationships and high/low context, bringing to the fore entrenched cultural mores generally excluded from economic analysis. The integration of the relational access dimension with the matrix thus transforms communal views of the firm into a holistic model of Japanese intra- and interfirm relationships, and the first priority of this model is the necessity to place all relationships along an *uchi–soto* (insider–outsider) continuum.

The r-dimension of the *uchi–soto* continuum defines where one firm stands in relationship to another firm—from the center of group membership to the outermost sphere of the spot transactional market (no relationship). In addition, in some contexts, a firm can be an insider because it is within a larger sphere while simultaneously an outsider, depending on its relative position within the concentric spheres of relationships surrounding any Japanese firm. Table 3.1 describes the characteristics of the insider–outsider continuum.

Figure 3.3   The relational access paradigm: the third dimension

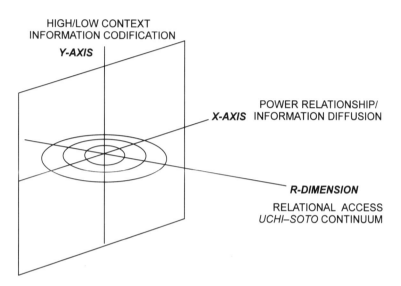

According to our paradigm, relationships follow a graded pattern based on a concentric, rather than a linear-contractual model; individuals are located in a work group, within the firm, situated in a industrial group, within a larger society. (See Figure 3.4.) For example, when applied to the *keiretsu* system (as illustrated in Figure 3.2), this graded system of relationships serves as an important distancing mechanism which excludes obligational relations of prime contractors from the affiliates of their subcontractors. This

Table 3.1   Characteristics of the insider–outsider continuum

Insider (Uchi)	*Outsider* (Soto)
Access to other insiders	No relationship
Protection from outsiders	Competition
Obligations within sphere	No obligations

has had enormous implications in terms of the hollowing-out of Japanese industry in recent years as primary contractors have expanded their outsourcing of parts production overseas, abandoning their supplier networks in Japan.

In Chapters 4 and 5 we will discuss in more detail the origins and nature of industrial group relationships and how the characteristics of the different types correlate specifically to the *keiretsu*, which we see as subsidiary/feudal-like and asymmetrical in power in their interfirm relationships, and the *kigyo shudan*, which we characterize as collegial and synergistic.

In the contractual relationship model of the Western economic paradigm, the firm is described as a nexus of linear contracts in a freely negotiated market. The approach of transaction-cost analysis represents a continuum between two opposing idealized modes—the market mode versus the hierarchical mode. The approach of agency theory typically sees the firm as a nexus of linear contracts and is itself rooted in the concept of a bundle of freely marketable contractual rights embodied historically in the seventeenth-century Anglo-Dutch concept of the joint-stock company. Although claiming to be universalistic theories, both the transaction-cost and agency approaches (1) fail to account for some of the outstanding

Figure 3.4   *R*-dimension: relational access insider–outsider continuum

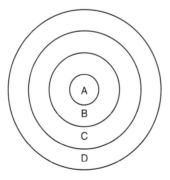

For example, in this illustration, Firms A and B are insiders in relationship to Firm C. Firm D is an outsider to Firms A and B. Firm C may have some kinds of relationships with Firm D because they border each other.

characteristics of the Japanese market, such as the quite notable lack of freedom, information, and transparency, *a priori* requirements for efficient marketplace theories to be relevant, and (2) ignore the social embeddedness of economic relations and transactions, the issues we deal with in our model.

In our view, the Japanese firm can be termed a "nexus of *implicit relational* contracts," indicative of its character as a high-context communal society. We argue that the theories of the firm promulgated by Western economists are caught in a mistaken and reductionist linearity. In our view the boundaries of the concept of the firm and group companies should be extended beyond those drawn by *de jure* property rights theories to encompass a concept of the firm and group as participants in an arena of collective action in which viability as an institution is greatly dependent on the supportive milieu in which the firm and its group are situated. In Japanese society a very different construction of collective relations is contained in the concept of "household" and the distinctions between family and firm as compared with the West. In Chapter 4 we will analyze the historical roots of the concept of the *ie*-style merchant household in Japan, arguing that the traditions and practices that took shape in the *ie*-group firms of long ago form the cultural basis for the intra- and interfirm relationships of Japanese governance structures today. These practices will provide evidence supporting the third dimension of our matrix, the insider–outsider continuum of relational access, characteristic of Japanese and other East Asian firms, and of high-context societies in general.

4 Origins of the Japanese Firm and Interfirm Networks

The organization of Japanese interfirm networks has received much attention over the last several years as a critical factor in Japan's economic success. Some have gone so far as to advocate the "keiretsu" group form as a model for U.S. and European industry, as well as developing economies, assuming that this organizational structure can be implemented simply as a policy choice. On the other hand, the lack of transparency of the interrelationships among firms, characteristic of Japanese groups, has become an issue in the ongoing trade negotiations between the U.S. and Japan, and it is thus no surprise that the U.S. side sees the existence of these group relationships as a major impediment to open markets.

Largely in reaction to rising external pressure, similar concern over the lack of transparency in business relations is also beginning to be voiced by Japanese in the academic and business worlds and in the press. Hitherto nonexistent issues of corporate governance and shareholder rights have newly thrust themselves into the consciousness of management through growing independent shareholder demands for changes in corporate dividend and voting policies. However, it can be argued that much of the criticized opaqueness of transactions, lack of accountability of management, and lack of access of foreign firms stems from entrenched cultural and legal antecedents within traditional Japanese society and is therefore intractable to short-term cure.

In fact, the unique qualities of industrial organization in Japan has been a favorite subject of study of both social scientists and economists. Organizational sociologists and cultural anthropologists have described Japan as a "community model" [Dore, 1987]; others have contrasted Japanese culture to Western culture as a "belonging model" versus a Western "contractual model" [Mito, 1992]; another as a model based on "obligational contractual

45

relations" versus an "arm's-length contractual relations" model [Sako, 1992]; and within the overall context of East Asian business systems, a Japanese model built on high trust communal relations of village and family and an aloof state [Whitley, 1992].

Noting the special character of Japanese-style capitalism, some sociologists and economists have called it "Network Capitalism" [Nakatani, 1990]; "Alliance Capitalism" [Gerlach, 1992]; or even "Beyond Capitalism" [Sakakibara, 1994]; or, by using game theory principles, have attempted to create a J-model [Aoki, 1984a]. Other economists studying Japanese society have taken a different approach, placing the firm within the context of established Western economic conceptualizations like agency theory [Aoki, 1984b, 1990; Sheard, 1989, 1991].

On the other hand, political scientist Chalmers Johnson [1982] dismisses both the economist's view for its "unique-structural-features" models as well as the social-anthropologist's view for its "national character-basic values-consensus" humanist models and, not surprisingly, weighs in with his own "Developmental State" model.

This lack of fit between the terms of debate in management theory led by economists and the observations made of Japanese management practice by sociologists, among others, may well reflect a fundamental clash between the bias of Western-trained theorists who wish to see their models as universal and the observations of those who, as much as possible, look at the Japanese firm without those constraints. In this chapter we will examine the evidence used in developing our theoretical construct, the Relational Access Paradigm, as it is rooted in the historical and cultural origins of the Japanese firm and the transformation of these firms into industrial groups.

HISTORICAL EVIDENCE: HOUSEHOLDS AS FIRMS

There is perhaps no more evocative word in the Japanese language than *ie*, most literally "family," which encompasses a range of meanings from simply "kinsfolk" to "dwelling" to a value-laden sense of "household." Historically shaped by Confucian familial rights and obligations, the word *ie* today still connotes the social basis of one's fundamental relationships—to parents and offspring, to community and workplace. By purposefully extending the household collective beyond relationships bound purely by blood, the *ie* has continued to serve from Japanese medieval times to the present as the basic unit of a cohesive social structure that eventually built the "Japanese economic miracle."

The *toyo kanji* (ideograph) for family, "*ie*", shown in Figure 4.1 below, illustrates its roots.

The ideograph consists of two elements: a roof over a pig, a domesticated animal in a dwelling. This image succinctly symbolizes the importance placed upon the household's economic role over the human aspects of a conjugal nuclear family. The conjugal nuclear family is subordinate to the *ie*. The *ie*'s significance as an economic collective has, in fact, brought added relevance to the word's other meanings.

The *ie* concept of the household unit may be traced back to ancient times and has its earliest roots in the cooperative nature of traditional agricultural production [Nakane, 1970]. Later, in the seventh century, Confucian concepts were imported from China and adapted by the elite classes, providing fundamental support for the *ie* ideology. Diffusion of Confucian ideas to all social orders did not occur until much later, during the Tokugawa period. Until then peasant family members were scattered as serfs among the noble classes within the feudal order [Nakane, 1990].

Confucian thought is an ethical system based on filial piety. Its primary emphasis is on duty and obligation in social and household relations within a hierarchically-oriented society. The historical focus of Confucian doctrine was the cult of the family [Matsumoto, 1960]. In general, it prescribed: (1) the hierarchical relations between members; (2) personal loyalty consisting of reciprocal duties and obligations; (3) ritual observances of these reciprocities; (4) contractual arrangements between groups patterned after family relationships [Bennett and Ishino, 1963].

Buddhism also entered Japan from China via Korea in the sixth century. Stressing *nirvana*, the losing of self in infinity—the efface-ment of ego—this doctrine of self-abnegation had a profound effect on Japanese culture. Its social impact through an emphasis on the cultivation of humility and the subordination of individual ambition for a collective good cannot be underestimated, particularly in regard to its implicit support for key Confucian values [Matsumoto, 1960]. Confucianism and Buddhism were complementary to the *ujigami*—patron deities of the native Shinto local-god system. Together the three evolved into a family religion, commonly referred to as ancestor worship, which had come to be virtually universal in Tokugawa Japan. The brief daily ceremony before the family shrine was a constant reminder to household members of their obligations to the *ie* [Bellah, 1957].

The *ie* was central to that doctrine, the most basic economic, political, and social collective unit of a society that was itself governed by precepts of *giri*, obligations and duties to superiors, and *on*, benevolence to inferiors. Within the *ie*, the most important criterion by which to evaluate action and behavior was how well it served the group. In such a collectively-oriented society, the indivi-dual hardly existed as a distinct entity, and failure to fulfill one's obligations was considered selfish, or even cowardly [M. Yoshino, 1968]. This *ie* ideological system suited Japan's oligarchic feudal system quite well. The *daimyo* (feudal lord) was referred to as *shushin* (lord-parent) and the followers as *ienoko* (children of the family). First adopted by the warrior class, the samurai, the *ie* house system later informed the business and social practices of the merchant and the artisan classes as these groups increased in economic importance.

The *giri* psychology of moral obligation and duty provided stability to the two-and-a-half centuries of peace and tranquillity of Tokugawa Japan, following a hundred years of civil wars—the *sengoku jidai* (epoch of wars), when feudal war lords battled each other for power and control [Matsumoto, 1960]. It was after the Battle of Sekigahara in 1600 that Tokugawa hegemony was estab-lished. Tokugawa Ieyasu carefully constructed a class structure that was to become largely immutable. Its rigid hierarchy, popularly known as the *shi-no-ko-sho* (warrior–farmer–artisan–merchant classes), declared the peasants second only to the samurai in the social pecking order, although they ranked last economically.

By the mid-1700s the whole of Japanese society was comprised of economic units based on households reinforced by a religious cult of the family. During this *Pax Tokugawa* every effort was made to suppress change in order to maintain the social structure. Tokugawa government policy sought to settle peasants permanently in stable villages and establish the *ie* as the basic unit of society. During the seventeenth and eighteenth centuries, land and tenant rights were promulgated among the peasantry making it possible for individual farming households to establish themselves. Family units could then remain intact through successive generations. Thus formalized by law, the peasantry began to adopt the family values of the samurai household codes [Nakane, 1990].

The *ie* was seen first and foremost as an ongoing enterprise rather than as a sanguineous family unit. Once an *ie* was established, its continuity through successive generations was of major concern to its members. If there was no son, a daughter's husband would be adopted into the household to assume the family name and eventually inherit the household. If there were no children at all, a son or daughter would be adopted and, with his or her spouse, carry on the household. Kinship blood ties were not as important as the suitability of the candidate to manage the affairs of the household, particularly in a merchant family. Although a son would normally be considered first choice to inherit, if unsuited to the task he might be sent to establish his own branch-household while a long-time faithful employee would be chosen as successor, married to a daughter, and adopted into the household [Nakane, 1990].

Although the laws of inheritance allowed for only one heir so as to preserve the property of the household, custom provided for the establishment of branch households for additional offspring and loyal apprentices who had become part of the *ie*. It is these last two attributes, the adoption of a non-blood member as heir and the indivisibility of inherited property, that distinguishes the Japanese institution of the *ie* from other East Asian family/kinship enterprise systems, such as in China and Korea [Pelzel, 1970; Hattori, 1984].

The harsh living conditions of the Tokugawa period made the division of property among offspring nearly impossible, so that only the wealthiest families were able to bestow any assets on a second or third son. However, this was not as major a problem as it may appear since the high mortality rates of the Tokugawa period continued all the way through the 1930s. This often meant that second or third sons could be adopted into other households in the same or neighboring villages. It is estimated that even today one third of Japanese households are headed by adopted sons-in-law [Nakane, 1990].

It was most common that, in the formative stages of the household enterprise, the direct management of the *ie* was in the hands of family members for the first two generations. As the business grew in stability and size, however, often by the third generation, competent managers who had grown up in the *ie* from early childhood and had been promoted from *detchi* to *tedai* then *banto* (apprentice, salesperson, manager), were ready to assume the management operations of an expanded business. It was often at this stage in the development of the *ie* that management of the *mise* (store) became physically separated from the *oku* (back living quarters), symbolically marking the progression from a nuclear family business to an extended family business. For *ie* that had grown to a very large scale, such as Mitsui, it was imperative that nonfamily-member managers be given authority since there could not possibly be a sufficiently large talent pool within the Mitsui family itself [Horie, 1977].

The *banto* (manager) was permitted to marry at age twenty-five and was then provided by the master with a *bekke* (separate house). Those who continued to work within the *honke* (main house) were guaranteed their livelihood after retirement. Those *bekke* that operated a business were financed and given a share of the goodwill by the *honke,* whether in the same or a different type of business. Apprentices for the main house were selected from the among the sons of the *bekke*, thus maintaining the fictive kinship relationship [Horie, 1977].

The collectivist-centered development of the Japanese firm was a result of and has been reinforced by cultural/religious traditions particular to Japan and different from the West. In contrast, the weakened role of the household firm in Western Europe is exemplified by the creation in early seventeenth-century England and the Netherlands of the joint-stock company form, whose main features included: (1) perpetual succession as an immortal legal entity; (2) legal separation of ownership from management; (3) the right to trade its common stock; (4) limited liability to its shareholders in its later development as a corporation.

The Japanese family firm in the *ie*-system was able to accomplish some of the same objectives while retaining the motivational aspects of a household business: (1) perpetuation of the firm by training of suitable successors from within the *ie*; (2) securing the loyalty of management to the household by the use fictive kinship status; (3) the indivisibility of the *ie* and its assets, which tended to constrain the ability of any one individual stakeholder to act on his own against the overall interests of the household.

THE TRANSFORMATION FROM MERCHANT HOUSEHOLDS TO INDUSTRIAL GROUPS

The previous section briefly traced the evolution of the *ie*-based form. In what follows it will be shown that the financial and personnel practices unique to Japanese corporations were formed in light of the historical legacy of the *ie*, which shaped the subsequent transformations of the firm and the development of industrial groups. We now consider three *ie* that gained considerable prominence in the twentieth century; their history not only exemplifies the evolution of the *ie*-form but also provides us with the framework for our examination of contemporary industrial group practices.

The origins of the *zaibatsu* and its successors the *keiretsu* and *kigyo shudan* are found in the establishment of the merchant family houses of the Tokugawa period [Yonekura, 1985]. The Konoike, Sumitomo, and Mitsui families present case histories of extended household enterprises or family associations which began as merchants in money-lending, metals mining and smelting, and the dry goods business, but which later developed into banking and industrial empires. These three household businesses are examples of the *dozoku* (extended family) consisting of a *honke* (main house), *bunke* (related branch house), and *bekke* (unrelated branch house). Although all three were engaged in different types of businesses and strategies, each developed the capital resources and a household enterprise management system during the early Tokugawa period that enabled them to continue to prosper during the industrialization era of the Meiji period.

After the consolidation of Tokugawa rule in the beginning of the seventeenth century, a need arose to supply tribute and to provide funds and goods for the enforced residence of the *daimyo* (feudal lords) families held hostage by the Tokugawa shogun in Edo (present-day Tokyo). To facilitate this trade new national commercial centers sprang up in the cities of Osaka, Edo, seat of the military government, and in Kyoto, the imperial capital. Osaka became the greatest entrepôt, not only for the tax rice, but also for the products of the monopolies of the various *han* (fiefdoms), such as cotton cloth, rapeseed oil, paper, sugar, salt, wax, and iron ore. By the end of the seventeenth century, some ninety-five daimyo rice warehouses had been established in Osaka to receive shipments from the provinces. Through these activities Tokugawa Japan developed a monetarized commodity economy [Sakudo, 1990].

In the scheme of things in the pre-Tokugawa period, principally 1580 to 1610, the feudal lords had set up castle towns in each of their domains. Commerce flourished there to provide goods and services for the lords and their samurai retainers who were required to reside in the town. Peasants brought their handicrafts to sell to the merchants and to buy the few necessities that they could afford. The merchants chiefly provided exchange services to the samurai, exchanging their rice stipends for cash, and supplying their other needs as well. In time these small family businesses became the prototypes for the merchant family houses in the major consumer centers of Osaka, Kyoto, and Edo [Nakane, 1990].

Osaka became the central commodity market for the whole country, handling the tax rice business of the shogun and daimyo. Well-suited for the task, Osaka was conveniently situated near Kyoto, where the imperial court resided, near Nara, the former capital, and near Hyogo (modern Kobe), also a port since ancient times, and it possessed as well a long history as a center for domestic and international trade. In the seventeenth century, as Osaka developed into the center of Japan's economy, a new class of merchants arose to handle the brokerage of the growing tax rice trade. From their exchange houses, this merchant group increasingly focused on money lending, providing loans to the powerful daimyo, with the tax rice shipments as collateral, thereby laying the foundations for the growth of their own economic power [Sakudo, 1990].

Although agriculture was the basis of the economy, and the farmer class nominally held the next highest social station below the samurai, in fact over 40% of the farmer's output was taken in taxes by the ruling lords. During the 250 years of peace of the Tokugawa period, however, the *raison d'être* of the samurai as a warrior caste ceased to exist except to enforce the feudal status quo. Comprising 6% of the population, they became little more than a parasitic class which received its fixed annual rice stipend from the taxes levied on the farmers, serving only as an hereditary class of administrators for the great lords, the daimyo [Matsumoto, 1960].

Lowest in status were the merchants, comprising another 6% of the population (together with the artisans), but as a class they wielded great economic influence, and, together with the lower-ranking samurai, provided much of the impetus for change towards the end of the Tokugawa period in the early nineteeth century [Matsumoto, 1960]. The merchant class climbed in prominence and economic power as the main economic concern of the feudal great lords was no longer how to provision an army but how to raise enough cash to cover the heavy expenses their status and obligatory court attendance required. Inevitably the daimyo were forced to turn to the merchants, particularly of Osaka, for the commercial services mentioned above, such as the storage and marketing of tax rice, and for lines of credit when and where required. The merchants, in turn, evolved an elaborate code of ethical rules and conduct for themselves, paralleling the intricate rules of conduct of the samurai class whose influence they were gradually replacing in Japanese society [M. Yoshino, 1968].

The Sumitomo merchant house was founded in Kyoto in the sixteenth century and became a smelting house for silver and copper, a technology learned from Western traders by the house's founder Sumitomo Masatomo in 1591. By the third generation the house had expanded into banking after opening a money-changing store in Osaka [Horie, 1966; Sakudo, 1990].

It is interesting to note that whatever the core business of the great household enterprises, there was always a financial branch, i.e., an exchange house or money-lending branch of the enterprise, the forerunner of the modern *kigyo* group-affiliated bank, which contributed to the monetatization of the early Tokugawa economy. The five main houses of the Mitsui family businesses were organized under the leadership of Echigoya Hachiroemon, the *soryoke* (senior house) head of the *dozoku*, who controlled the Mitsui dry goods stores in Kyoto, Osaka, and Edo as well as the group's *omotokata* (central business office). The other main houses were the Mitsui Money-Changing Stores, which were headed by Mitsui Saburosuke in Kyoto, Mitsui Motonosuke in Osaka, and Mitsui Jiroemon in Edo. In addition, affiliated houses were headed by the descendants and relatives of the founder of the house, Mitsui Takatoshi. By the early eighteenth century, the Mitsui family consisted of nine houses, one senior, five main, three affiliated; two additional houses were later added so that by the time of the dissolution of the Mitsui *zaibatsu* after World War II by the Allied Occupation authorities an eleven-house structure was in place [Horie, 1966].

The Mitsui family business had begun as a dry-goods store in Edo in the latter part of the seventeenth century. The family founder moved his dry-goods store in 1683 to a new location and embarked upon innovative sales techniques which included cash sales at cheaper pre-marked prices, the use of colorful advertising broadsides, and the nationwide wholesaling of goods to retailers. Also that year a money-changing store was established, and in 1691 the household was appointed official merchants to the shogun's government with authorization to handle the conversion of gold and silver notes issued by the government [Yonekura, 1985].

In 1705 a Mitsui family council was established to control the dry-goods stores in Edo, Kyoto, and Osaka; in 1710 a central business office was created for all their enterprises; and in 1719 a family banking council was set up to oversee the operation of their money-changing shops in the three cities. After the death of Takatoshi in 1694, the business leadership was passed on to his four sons who maintained a joint ownership and group leadership in the extended family council. The distribution of the Mitsui *dozoku's* collective assets were codified in the Mitsui Family Bylaws of 1722 [Horie, 1966; Mitsui Gomei-Kaisha, 1933].

At the head of the Mitsui household structure was the *omotokata* (central business office) which was governed by a council of house heads. The *omotokata* would advance investment capital and working capital to each enterprise in the group, which semiannually would repay a fixed percentage of the advance, reflecting the earnings of each store, and averaging a 12% return on the funds advanced. Each enterprise was financially independent and had discretion over the use of its own funds. Although outwardly similar in structure to a modern holding company and its affiliated enterprises, the *omotokata* had unlimited liability for the management of each enterprise so the relationship was in fact more like that between a company and its subsidiary [Sakudo, 1990].

The process of establishing house rules began for the Konoike family in 1614 when founder Yamanaka Shinroku wrote down his precepts for managing the *ie*. Masatomo, founder of the Sumitomo family, also inscribed for perpetuity his admonitions for business activities before his death in 1652. Mitsui Takatoshi first codified his collected precepts in 1673, with amendments in 1675 and 1676. By the eighteenth century, the Konoike, Sumitomo, and Mitsui families all had well-established house rules. The common features these codes shared included: the centrality of the main house in relation to the branch houses; admonitions against speculative, risk-taking activities; and the promotion of frugality and businesslike accounting procedures. The rules stipulated collective business decision-making through deliberative councils and consultation, and rejected individual and arbitrary rulemaking [Mitsui Gomei-Kaisha, 1933; Miyamoto, 1984].

The personnel practices of the Mitsui house were prototypic of the household system of management that developed in the eighteenth century. Although it was thought desirable that all employees be raised from infancy within the *ie*, outside apprentices were allowed in if suitably young. Furthermore, in the Kyoto store, for example, the apprentice had to come from a community at least 60 kilometers away. Sixteen different ranks were established, from apprentice to foremen, administrators, and managers, and until 1735 seniority was the sole basis of promotions. After that, performance also became a criterion for advancement for employees above the rank of foreman [Sakudo, 1990].

The Konoike family, prominent in the money-lending business, created a compulsory retirement savings plan that provided the capital resources for employees to establish their own businesses. In the Mitsui house, employees who remained until they attained high rank could also be allowed to open a *bekke*, or branch house, and use the firm's logo [Sakudo, 1990]. This network formation prefigured the creation of the modern-day industrial groups.

CULTURE, COMMERCE, AND COMMUNAL VALUES

The social foundation which enabled the development of the merchant household-style business was based, as earlier detailed, on a distinctive concept of kinship. Although some Western scholars have credited Western influence for the successes of Japanese industrial management, the management styles so notable today are in fact rooted in the history of non-blood, fictive kinship-based economic units—the merchant "household-style" business unit. This concept of fictive kinship relationships was firmly established by the mid-Tokugawa period of the eighteenth century and provided the basis for the distinctive Japanese long-term employment system, job advancement, and paternalism, characteristics of the management stability of modern Japanese industry. Similarly, today's corporate enterprise group (*kigyo shudan*) and affiliated group (*keiretsu*) relationships may be seen as the direct descendants of the *ie*-branch system of affiliated households, in which managers were allowed to open affiliated branches, *bekke* and *bunke,* of the main household, *honke*.

Kinship is a phenomenon considered important in tribal societies but assumed to be of little importance in an industrial society by economists, who thus have tended to overlook critical aspects of the social embeddedness of economic relations and transactions [Granovetter, 1985]. This is particularly true of Japan where, for example, simulated kinship roles were not only of much importance in traditional occupations but continue in modern managerial practices as well [Bennett and Ishino, 1963].

The inter-generational character of the family, exemplified in the paternalistic *oyabun–kobun* (parent status–child status) relationship, is yet another aspect of the *ie* (household) construct that underpins relationship patterns within Japanese businesses and Japanese society as a whole. In general, this relationship resembles the elements of Max Weber's description of patrimonial bureaucracy in his *Wirtschaft und Gesellschaft* (*Theory of Social Economic and Organization*) [Weber, 1921/1947]. However, *oyabun–kobun* goes well beyond Weber's mentor–student or master–apprentice relationship, by carrying with it an extensive web of interlocking obligations and duties called *on* and *giri* which pose a distinct contrast to the Western formulation of personal "rights and privileges." It is the reciprocity inherent in *oyabun-kobun* that binds the Japanese *kumi* (group) together, whether it be a team or guild, a company or even a corporation [Bennett and Ishino, 1963].

Japanese relationships generally follow a graded pattern based on a concentric, rather than linear-contractual, model in which the household is located within the community within the larger country (*kuni*). In this Confucian-influenced system the household, whether based on blood or fictive relations such as the Japanese *ie*, is situated within a *mura* (village), and in the case of the firm within its *kigyo shudan*. (See Figure 3.4 from our earlier discussion of insider–outsider relationships.) In our later discussion of governance, this multi-tiered framework will prove to be important to where we place the bank in relationship to the firm. Such sets of graded concentric relationships are grounded on the distinctions between the role of *uchi* (insiders) versus *soto* (outsiders), whom Japanese refer to as *kankeinai hito*—persons with whom one has no relationship and who therefore may be disregarded. (See Figure 4.2 below for this Japanese Confucian-influenced system.)

The basic framework of the household system rests upon a tradition in which non-blood-related individuals function together as a simulated kinship group [M. Yoshino, 1968]. Even when the internal structure of a modern industrial enterprise grows beyond a small-sized business, traditional patterns of *on* and *giri* continue. Subsidiaries and sub-units assume the traditional obligations to their employees [Bennett and Ishino, 1963]. Similarly, the traditional distinctions between insider and outsider are in play in the modern notion of the "lifetime employee," a modern-day embodiment of the traditional apprentice, an adoptive member of the *ie* (household). Today the most sought-after jobs for new university graduates are those not only with a prestigious company but also with a secure "family" culture. Only some 30% of Japanese industrial workers are considered to have "lifetime" status; an employee may still be

Figure 4.2   The Japanese Confucian-influenced system
of graded relationships

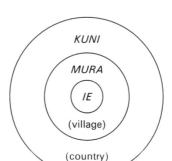

classified as "temporary " or "part-time" even after working twenty
years for the firm. The so-called temporary employee remains
outside the network of reciprocities, without the expectation of a
supportive *oyabun–kobun* relationship, "apprentice" status, a
"share" in the *ie,* or job security.

The attributes of modern Japanese-style management, such as the
lifetime employment system, promotion by seniority, and a paternalistic policy towards employees, have their historical basis in the
annals of medieval seventeenth-century merchant households. These
household codes governing the management of family businesses
contained specific regulations on the theory and practice of long-
term employment, seniority, and the good treatment of employees
[Horie, 1966; Mitsui Gomei-Kaisha, 1933; Miyamoto, 1984; Sakudo,
1990].

In our view, the process of modernization in Japan may be
viewed, in some very fundamental aspects, as the continuous development of native institutions rather than as the result of the abrupt
introduction of Western ideas in the Meiji period of the late nineteenth century. Today, the values and beliefs associated with the *ie*
(household) concept are alive not only in family-operated businesses
but are reflected in the relationships and practices within firms and
within industrial groups, whether horizontally or vertically structured. The traditional access given within one's extended *ie* are now

given to those of one's group. The values placed on personal relationships implied in the informal channels of communication are indicative of the importance of a shared culture and value system.

5 Japanese Governance Structures in the Postwar Era: Industrial Groups and Their Main Banks

The governance of modern Japanese firms and industrial organizations has been much studied and debated—both mechanistically and qualitatively. Studies taking a structural approach have focused on group boundaries [Gerlach, 1992], others have studied bureaucratic influence [Schaede, 1993, 1994], while still others have taken a contractual approach in their analysis [Gilson and Roe, 1993]. Hadley [1970], Aoki [1987] and Miyajima [1994] each provide a history of the transformation from prewar *zaibatsu* to postwar industrial groups. Some economists suggest that the group operates to distribute risk-sharing among the members [Nakatani, 1984; Aoki, 1984b]. Two issues stand out as key concerns in the debate on governance structures: the implications of cross-shareholding and the role of the main bank.

It should be noted here that a number of Japanese studies have explored these same areas but have gone largely unnoticed in Western literature. These include research on the effect, if any, of cross-shareholding upon stock prices [Ikeo, 1993; Kanesaki, 1986; Kawakita, 1992, 1993; Kobayashi, 1991, 1992; Kumagai, 1994; Kurasawa, 1984; Ogishima, 1993; Wakasugi, 1982] and cross-shareholding from corporate governance perspectives [Ito, 1993; Nomura Sogo Kenkyujo, 1992; and Okumura, 1990b]. Two recent studies by Japanese research teams have analyzed management attitudes towards cross-shareholding based on corporate survey responses [Omura, 1993; and Fuji Sogo Kenkyujo, 1993], focusing in particular on the firm's relationship with its main bank. Typically, none of the results of these Japanese studies have been included in discussions of Japanese industrial organization by the proponents of agency theory or, for that matter, by most other scholars outside of Japan.

INDUSTRIAL GROUPS: CROSS-SHAREHOLDING AND GROUP BOUNDARIES

Cross-Shareholding

Kabushiki mochiai—mutual aid shareholding, is the Japanese term for what is antiseptically, but customarily, translated as "cross-shareholding," that is, bilateral shareholding through which two companies hold stakes in one another. In 1987, cross-shareholdings represented 15.2% of the outstanding corporate stock issued in Japan by nonfinancial companies and some 22.7% when financial institutions are included [Japan Fair Trade Commission, 1989]. Cross-shareholdings, in turn, are a subset of what is known as *antei kabunushi*—quiescent stable shareholdings, held in trilateral, multilateral, or otherwise stable arrangements between companies, usually based on group and/or transactional relationships. Together, cross- and stable shareholdings comprise some 65% to 70% of all stock issued by publicly traded corporations in Japan. The remaining minority of shares are freely traded on the stock exchanges.

As we will show, however, cross-shareholding, when applied to Japan, describes more than a single-dimension ownership relationship and masks a culturally loaded connotation to those familiar with only its superficial meaning. The tacit mutual agreements that are often the real purpose of cross-shareholding are intended to avoid rather than confer shareholder rights. Designed to insulate management from any market threat of hostile takeover, the existence of the stable shareholding relationship is an essentially *anti*-corporate governance strategy.

For purposes of governance analysis, cross-shareholding may be divided into two categories: (1) cross-shareholding between members of an industrial group, or *kigyo shudan*, the core of stable shareholding arrangements, and (2) cross-shareholding that is indicative of business relationships between suppliers and customers. In the latter case, cross-shareholding arrangements are primarily a franchise to do business, a method of cementing transactional relationships. In neither case, however, is the cross-shareholding intended to confer the ownership rights inherent in the Anglo-American model of corporate governance. It is also within this second category of transactional relationships that a bank's shares of cross-held stock with its major business client firms should be viewed. The same is true for insurance companies and trust banks which typically own shares in companies with which they do a significant amount of business, including selling insurance and pension fund products to the client firm and its employees. Such transaction-related shareholdings are considered to be separate and apart from any holdings in the client firm's equity that these financial institutions may have in their investment portfolios.[4] We discuss in more detail in Chapter 6 the type of transactional business relationship that financial institutions have with their client firms and their employees.

A third type of corporate shareholding exists which is unrelated to issues of corporate governance. It is a form of speculative financial investment within a firm's investment portfolio that was particularly popular during the "bubble period" of credit-induced asset price inflation of the late 1980s. Known then as *zaitech*, or financial engineering, such investments characterized a period when companies believed that financial investing would yield a greater return than their core businesses. It is only in this last category of shareholding that there has been any show of the selling of shares, primarily to cover losses on a firm's P/L statement.

Failure to Distinguish Between *Kigyo Shudan* and *Keiretsu*

Further complicating and often confusing discussion relating to Japanese governance has been the steady agglomeration of terminology, which has made defining the boundaries between reciprocal, inclusive relationships and competitive market relationships all the

---

[4] In the author's interviews with trust bank and insurance executives, they reported that they principally rely on fixed-income securities in their investment portfolios to meet their actuarial needs, and that the overwhelming percentage of client firm equities being held were for "relational" purposes.

more difficult. This expansion of inaccurate vocabulary has led not only to the misuse of terms but in some cases to incorrect inferences. For example, Nakatani [1983] (as well as many other Japanese scholars), when writing in Japanese use the correct usage "*kigyo shudan*," but incorrectly substitute "*keiretsu*" in the English version of their articles [Nakatani, 1984]. Gerlach [1992], as another example, imposes the use of the term "*keiretsu*" for a general description for all types of industrial groups. This acquiescence to misuse in nomenclature inevitably and predictably has popularized a mistake that is perpetuated by numerous scholars, journalists, and government officials, resulting in the blurring and misunderstanding of important issues. The distinction between the *kigyo shudan* and *keiretsu* is important because the nature of the power relationships and relational access, as earlier described, is not the same.

Such misconstruing of *keiretsu* and *kigyo shudan*, by sheltering from scrutiny the formal and informal governance structures based on principles of relational access, leave issues such as lack of transparency and lack of information inadequately examined. For example, in 1992 Japan's Economic Planning Agency (JEPA) felt compelled to respond to U.S. criticism raised in the Strategic Structural Initiative (SSI) trade negotiations that cross-shareholding promoted unfair trading practices. Characterizing them as "merits," the JEPA advanced three main economic justifications, among others, for cross-shareholding.

It argued that cross-shareholding provides a stable source of funding for businesses by ensuring partners who will be stable investors and who will buy new issues of stock whenever needed. Furthermore, according to the JEPA, cross-shareholding strengthens the stability of corporate management by acting as a bulwark against the threat of hostile takeover. Such arrangements relieve management of the necessity of responding to excessive pressures from the capital markets, permitting it to develop operations according to a long-term perspective. Lastly, the JEPA maintained, cross-shareholding stabilizes and strengthens business transactions between companies. The JEPA White Paper of 1992 termed cross-shareholding a mutual "hostage" taking, which creates a captive relationship in the supply of goods or services and promotes long-term transactional relationships between cross-shareholding companies.

The extent of cross-shareholding within the group's companies is often pointed to, particularly from abroad, as a measure of exclusionary, anti-competitive business practices in view of the fact that group companies tend to do business mainly with each other, thus discouraging foreign investment in Japan, as was pointed out at the Strategic Structural Initiative negotiations.

It is interesting to note that, while promoting these particular "merits," the Economic Planning Agency also conceded:

> Even though interlocking stockholding has the functions mentioned above, if it creates a relationship of "conspiracy," business may become inefficient. What is more important, in selecting the customers, if it is taken into account whether or not they have interlocking stockholding unrelated to their individual products or substance of service, or cartel relations come into existence between competitors, competition may be limited. [Japan Economic Planning Agency, 1992, p. 181]

As we shall see, cross-shareholding arrangements spring from concepts of relational access in which such effects as anti-competitive practices and lack of management accountability are protected through reliance on principles of an *uchi–soto* continuum.

THE RESURRECTION AND EVOLUTION OF CROSS-SHAREHOLDING IN THE POSTWAR PERIOD

The modern origins of today's cross-shareholding arrangements may be traced to the dissolution of the prewar *zaibatsu* in the initial period of the Allied occupation of Japan following World War II. The dissolution of the *zaibatsu* holding companies was intended to introduce Western principles of economic democracy and to dismantle the industrial underpinnings of Japanese militarism. The forced divestiture of the *zaibatsu* of their corporate holdings by the Anti-Trust Act of 1949 led to an increase in stock ownership by individual investors; as a result, individual investors held 69.1% of all outstanding shares by 1949.

The postwar cross-shareholding system developed in three periods: the first in the early 1950s, the second from the middle 1960s to early 1970s, and the third in the late 1980s. The period of the early 1950s was characterized by an active takeover market and free-wheeling shareholder meetings. It was during this period, as speculators purchased stocks, forcing management to buy back their stock at a higher price (greenmail), that companies tried to protect themselves by cross-shareholding. However, the original provisions of the Anti-Trust Act prohibited stockholding by companies. Revision of the Act in 1953 allowed companies to invest in stocks providing their stock holdings could not be construed as anti-competitive. The resurrection of cross-shareholding during this period was primarily intended to protect companies from unsolicited acquisition by speculators after the collapse of Japanese stock prices in the aftermath of Japan's economic boom during the Korean War. The 1953 easing of the Anti-Trust Act also raised the upper limit of holdings by financial institutions from 5% to 10%.

It was during this first period in the development of cross-shareholding of the 1950s that the former *zaibatsu* groups of Sumitomo, Mitsui, and Mitsubishi reestablished themselves as *kigyo shudan*, with their trading companies and banks at the center of their groups.

The next major change took place during the second period from the mid-1960s to early 1970s. This change was precipitated by the collapse of share prices in 1964–65 and the subsequent Yamaichi Crisis, in which Japan's fourth largest securities company was faced with imminent bankruptcy. In order to boost the Japanese market a special corporation, the Nihon Kyodo Shoken (Japan Cooperative Securities Co.), was set up by the securities industry with Ministry of Finance (MoF) "guidance" to make major purchases of shares. It was staffed by MoF *amakudari* (Ministry retirees who are referred to as having "descended from heaven") and temporarily reassigned MoF personnel. In addition, in 1964 Japan had become a member of the Organization for Economic Cooperation and Development. As a condition of membership, Japanese capital markets were to be gradually deregulated, causing the Ministry of Finance as well as business to become concerned about preventing hostile takeovers by foreign investors.

Once the Yamaichi crisis had been averted, the Nihon Kyodo Shoken proceeded to sell the shares it had accumulated to group-linked companies and their banks, eliminating any potential threat of hostile takeovers by either domestic or foreign investors. Section #280 of the Commercial Act was revised so that boards of companies would be able to acquire additional capital and allocate newly issued shares to specified companies and individuals. Such allocations were primarily to financial institutions and companies within their own group, resulting in further stabilization and concentration of stock ownership. As a result, not only were the former prewar *zaibatsu* groups strengthened, but the development of the newly emerging postwar *kigyo shudan*, which were centered around Sanwa, Dai-Ichi Kangyo Bank (DKB), and Fuji[5] banks, was also significantly aided.

Following Japan's first "Oil Shock" in the fall of 1973, and after much opposition, the Fair Trade Commission moved to reduce bank shareholding of company stocks from 10% to 5% in an attempt to combat large-scale opportunistic price-hiking by corporations. The implementation of this reform took ten years, following the final passage of the 1977 Anti-Monopoly Reform Bill.

During the period of the late 1980s, the so-called "bubble period," corporations flooded the equities market with new issues. In this period the primary purpose of cross-shareholding was to prevent a decrease in the ratio of stable shareholders and to provide some stability to stock prices in the secondary market. This was also a period of intensive *zaitech* speculative investment in securities by corporations, unrelated to investment for cross-shareholding purposes. The portfolio of the *zaitech* investor, like any unaffiliated investor, was strictly speculative, generally taken in the form of *tokkin* accounts, that is, discretionary trusts managed by their brokers.

---

[5] Although Fuji Bank's so-called Fuyo group originated before the war as the Yasuda group of financial companies, it was not a fully developed *zaibatsu*, since during the prewar period it lacked an industrial manufacturing base. Member companies of the Kawasaki and the Furukawa groups, both smaller former *zaibatsu*, now belong to the DKB group, thus leaving Sanwa, the only bank without any *zaibatsu* past, with the sobriquet "The People's Bank."

CROSS-SHAREHOLDING: GOVERNANCE OR ANTI-GOVERNANCE?

Agency theorists have based their analysis of corporate governance on their interpretation of three components, alleged congruents of cross-shareholding, that they argue are the essential monitoring elements of governance in the Japanese context: (1) the Presidents Association of the *kigyo shudan*—the *shacho-kai*; (2) the monitoring function of the main bank; and (3) the appointment of former bankers as outside directors to client firms as monitors. We examine the first point in this section, and points two and three in our discussion of the role of the main bank in later sections. We conclude that the agency theorists' ascription of monitoring powers to these mechanisms stems primarily from a lack of understanding as to the function and purpose they actually serve. Furthermore, the agency myth surrounding these components as governance mechanisms is challenged in Chapters 6 and 7 by quantitative empirical studies on corporations done by Japanese research teams, as well as by the author's own field research on Japanese banks, the very institutions which agency theorists contend have been delegated the primary monitoring role in Japanese corporate governance.

Kigyo Shudan Affiliation

Among the largest *kigyo shudan*, namely, those affiliated with the top six city banks, a distinction should be drawn between groups such as Mitsui, Mitsubishi, and Sumitomo, which are the direct descendants of the prewar *zaibatsu* of the same names, and groups which are affiliated with Dai-Ichi Kangyo, Sanwa, and Fuji Banks. Within the former, that is, the pre-war *zaibatsu* groups, the extent of cross-shareholding is far higher, 27.46% in 1989, with group members considering their trading company or the original core company within their group as the group's center, although the group's bank also plays a significant role. Group identity and loyalties are thought to be far stronger among the more tradition-bound former *zaibatsu* groups than they are in the postwar bank-centered DKB, Sanwa, and Fuji *kigyo shudan*, where group identity and cross-shareholding are far weaker, 15.83% in cross-held shares in 1989 according to JEPA calculations. Within all of the *kigyo shudan*, however, the group's bank and other financial institutions, together with the group's trading company, have the most global ties with all of the other group members by virtue of the basic nature of their transactional business.

Although the six largest *kigyo shudan* have been the most studied and analyzed, other significant groups exist, for example, around such banks as the Industrial Bank of Japan (IBJ), the largest of the long-term credit banks, or client firms of the Tokai Bank, based in the Nagoya region. Indeed, there are many other groups of lesser size associated with smaller city banks which have a strong regional base, or the regional banks themselves, and the second-tier regional (formerly *sogo* or mutual) banks, all of which have their "groups." It is the communal nature of Japanese society to coalesce in groups, and it is hard to imagine that any entity in Japan no matter how small its size does not consider itself to be a member of some group or another.

Presidents Association: The Shacho-kai

A common way of identifying firm membership in a particular *kigyo shudan* is by its membership in the group's *shacho-kai*, or Presidents Association.[6] Some scholars have chosen to translate *shacho-kai* as Presidents Club or Council. However, the Presidents Association is not a club in the usual social sense. Membership is solely ex officio and lasts only during the member's tenure as a president of a group company. Nor is it a council as has also been suggested. The word "council" implies a more deliberative function than actually transpires. Unsubstantiated assumptions as to the nature of the *shacho-kai*, apparently arising from the very existence of these organiza-

---

[6] The various *shacho-kai* groups meet monthly, and most are anonymously named by the day of the month they meet: Kinyo-kai—Friday Association (Mitsubishi); Nimoku-kai—Second Thursday Association (Mitsui); Sansui-kai—Wednesday Association (Sanwa); Sankin-kai—Third Friday Association (DKB); Fuyo Club (Fuji); and Hakusui-kai—White Water Society (Sumitomo).

tions, has led some agency theorists to suggest that the *shacho-kai* plays a significant role in corporate governance [see for example: Aoki, 1987; Sheard 1989, 1991]. The monthly meeting of the *shacho-kai* clearly does provide a venue for relationship building that is essential to conducting business. Indeed, the necessity of having a "relationship" is a *sine qua non* for conducting ongoing business in Japan. However, it would be considered indelicate, if not impertinent, for the *shacho-kai* to discuss its concerns about the business of a particular company, much less to assume the collective right to exercise its influence on a company's management.

In general, the actual activities at meetings of the *shacho-kai* have not been reported upon, although some banker respondents conjectured that the meetings often feature educational presentations, primarily as a context for the meeting's real purpose of networking. Yet, the myth of *"shacho-kai* governance" persists on the strength of the highly publicized "Mitsukoshi incident," as several respondents labeled this 1982 affair. When the Mitsukoshi department store's board of directors sought the resignation of their president for alleged thievery and fraud, they enlisted the aid of an "outside" Mitsukoshi director, a former member of the Mitsui *shacho-kai* to compel the president's departure. He, as well other members of the Mitsui *shacho-kai* acted to end the public embarrassment that had arisen over the Mitsukoshi president's misdeeds. The Mitsui group leaders were concerned not with economic motives but rather to avoid further besmirching of the venerable Mitsui group name by the recalcitrant Mitsukoshi president who was refusing to resign. This singular case has been summoned up ever since as an example of *"shacho-kai* governance." (See the discussion in Chapter 6 of such self-serving lore.) Yet, even in this case, it should be noted that the outside director and others reportedly acted only at the Mitsukoshi board's instigation, rather than taking the initiative themselves.

Cross-Shareholding as Anti-Governance

Not surprisingly, the prevalent view of scholars in Japan is that cross-shareholding is intrinsically *anti*-governance. There, critics have characterized the anti-governance effects of Japanese-style cross-shareholding as "demerits," particularly in terms of management accountability and anti-competitive practices.

For example, with no effective oversight by shareholders of corporate operations and managerial performance, until recently Japanese managers have had little incentive to manage efficiently beyond their self-interested need to perpetuate the company. In the U.S., because shareholders, at least theoretically, oversee the effectiveness of corporate management, the possibility exists of shareholders exercising their rights to change management if operations become inefficient. Corporate management is thus incentivized to have an interest in the more effective operation of the company for the benefit of the shareholders [Ito, 1993]. However, because of the mutual non-interference agreements generally implied in a Japanese cross-shareholding relationship, Japanese corporate management is given a superabundance of discretion in making business decisions and in regulating itself. This lack of monitoring leads to inefficiencies that produce a low return on equity, since declaring shareholder dividends is neither a necessity nor even a priority concern to corporate managers [Nomura Sogo Kenkyujo, 1992].

Critics in Japan also argue that the nature of cross-shareholding agreements can damage and even defraud shareholders. Viewed benignly, cross-shareholding merely represents an offsetting exchange of stock between companies, giving no advantage in funding because there is no injection of new outside capital. Only if equity financing is done at separate times and differing amounts of capital are raised will there be some limited merit for one side or the other. From the perspective of a third-party shareholder, however, these transactions can be seriously misleading. For example, normally when a company issues stock for ¥100 million in capital, the company then would end up owning assets worth ¥100 million. However, in a cross-shareholding arrangement, when one company issues stock to raise capital, there are no proceeds, just the receipt of new stock in exchange; the transaction is a purely paper one. The third-party investor may thus be defrauded either because he does not receive capital or because he has decided to invest based upon the belief that there is actually that amount of capital in the company when, in fact, there is only paper [Okumura, 1990b]. It is an unspoken fear that the consequences of any large-scale sell-off of shares by a cross-shareholding partner, without either consultation or the replacement of that partner with another stable shareholder, could bring about the general collapse of the company's shares in the equity market.

Cross-shareholding has also been criticized as having a negative effect on the stock market. It is argued that cross-shareholding will lead to fewer shares being traded on the exchange or in the secondary market. In other words, because the stocks of cross-held companies have a greater volatility in price, speculators can manipulate the market more easily. Such speculation in the Japanese stock market tends to discourage the trust of outside investors, and, in overall terms, would cause longer-term investors to leave the market.

Analysts taking the contrary view maintain, however, that under the efficient market hypothesis of the Miller–Modigliani Theorem, stock price fundamentals are based upon the net value of the company, and cross-shareholding should not affect the company's value, and therefore the ultimate effect of cross-shareholding upon stock prices remains neutral [Ikeo, 1993]. Still other analysts believe it has positive effect on price/earnings ratios [Ogishima, 1993], and some 82% of company executives surveyed held the belief that cross-shareholding has a beneficial effect in stabilizing their own company's stock price [Omura, 1993].

In fact, despite the apparently wide-spread consensus that cross-shareholding has either nil or a positive effect on stock prices, evidence shows cross-shareholding to have the opposite effect. The assets of companies holding cross-held stock are more vulnerable to share price volatility to the extent the company holds such stocks. This is because their corporate earnings ultimately tend to rely upon the stock prices of cross-held shares. If stock prices go up, the company earns "hidden profits" from these stocks, but if these stocks' prices go down, they will have unrealized losses. Japanese companies which showed a steady rise in their core business income between 1985 and 1991, suffered unrealized stock losses in cross-held shares when the stock market declined from 1989 to 1991. This resulted in an overall decline in their own company's stock price during those years, despite core business profits, to the extent that they held stock in cross-shareholding companies [Kawakita, 1992]. Thus, in this sense, their corporate earnings tend to depend upon cross-held stocks' prices.

INDUSTRIAL GROUPS AND
THE MAIN BANK RELATIONSHIP

Of all of a firm's cross-held relationships, one that has been among the most highly scrutinized is a firm's relationship with its main bank. A number of scholars have written on the history of the main bank system. Patrick [1967, 1983, 1994] outlined some of the history of the prewar banking period, and Horiuchi [1995] has given us an account of the wartime and postwar period. The main bank relationship, as it has come to be called in the past decade, is said by some to have had its origins in the 1930s when Japan's wartime economic planners sought to insure that companies deemed essential to the military economy received adequate funding for the uninterrupted production of munitions. Asajima [1984], studying *zaibatsu* group financing of the late 1930s, examined the Sumitomo group's shift of financing functions by its holding company to the group's bank and trust company. Teranishi [1994] pointed out the parallels between the role of the lead bank as part of a risk-diversification strategy for wartime loan syndication and in the postwar credit crunch period, while T. Okazaki [1994] emphasized the significance of the wartime planned economy and the National Mobilization Act. Nevertheless, as Horiuchi [1989] points out, when in 1944 the MoF ordered the 700 largest companies to specify their 'main banks,' the government was merely ratifying previously established de facto lead bank relationships.

Professor Yukio Noguchi [1995], a former MoF official, asserts that the Bank of Japan Law of 1942 was a conscious imitation of the Reichsbank Act promulgated in Nazi Germany in 1939. The argument he puts forward, which has since been echoed in official circles, academia, and the popular press, is that the current financial system is a product of the vicissitudes of the wartime economy, adapted to and reshaped by the requirements of postwar reconstruction, the result being an unfortunate legacy representing a marked aberration from the norm.

To the contrary, however, it was only the immediately preceding period, the post-World War I decade (1919–29), of free-wheeling financial markets that constituted an uncharacteristic departure from the historical norm. This laissez-faire period was characterized by economic chaos and bank failures that ultimately led to the

MoF's intervention in the 1927 bank crisis. Indeed, in historical terms, one can say that the government policy-based finance system has its oldest roots in the oligarchic rule of the Meiji *genro*, the "elder statesmen" period of the late nineteenth century, especially in the initiatives of Meiji Finance Minister Masayoshi Matsukata, who was noted for the autocratic control by which he successfully excluded any parliamentary authority and the involvement of any democratic processes as he constructed Japan's policy for economic development.

As T. Yoshino [1977] points out, contrary to the apocryphal stories regarding Japan's adoption of the Belgian model for its central bank, the Ministry of Finance in 1882, under the direction of Count Matsukata, after a rigorous process of examining the charters of more than thirty foreign central banks, decided upon the German model because it provided for the greatest control by the Ministry over the financial system, to the exclusion of parliamentary intervention. It is therefore not surprising, in view of the MoF's well-known predilection for maintaining autocratic control, that upon the expiration of the Bank of Japan's sixty-year old charter in 1942 the MoF would again look to the German model, which had been the basis of the old charter, for the BoJ's new charter.

Moreover, as we have seen from our earlier discussion in Chapter 4, it is in fact anti-historical to attempt to pinpoint the passage of any one government act or section of the Commercial Code as the foundation of modern-day bank–firm relationships. Such relationships not only predate the modern period but extend back in time to the exchange houses, the money lending stores, and the lending practices to group member houses of the *omotokata* (central business offices) of the great merchant households of the Tokugawa period.

Shareholding between the Japanese firm and its main bank is sometimes mistakenly compared to the German *Hausbank* system [see for example: Carrington and G. Edwards, 1979]. Indeed, there is a whole genre of literature, paralleling the literature on the Japanese main bank system, which favorably compares the *Hausbank*'s attributes to the market-based financing of the Anglo-American finance model and extols the purported efficiencies of German bank-based financing and bank monitoring [see for example: Cable, 1985; Crafts, 1992]. In the *Hausbank* system the bank is not only a shareholder but reportedly also exercises governance in the German two-tier board system by virtue of its dominant membership on the client firm's supervisory board of directors which it achieves through control of a substantial number of proxies. But here too, recent scholarship provides evidence that the outcome of such governance claims has been largely overstated [Baums, 1994; J. Edwards and Fischer, 1994]. In comparison, Japanese banks, though shareholders, are seldom in a position to influence policy, even in those firms in which they may hold outside directorships (*soto*). Typically, the Japanese firm's board of directors is made up of almost entirely of inside directors (*uchi*), that is, the firm's own executives, who are beholden to the president and chairman, both of whom retain real power along with the board's executive committee, also composed of inside directors.

Much of the present theorizing on the main bank relationship derives from a number of articles written by Nakatani on the purported governance/monitoring effects of the main bank within the industrial group. Nakatani puts forward the notion, first, that the industrial groups perform a risk-sharing function among their members, especially those grouped around a bank, which he sees as the group's center, and that the chief mechanism of that risk-sharing is the main bank's implicit assumption of the role of risk-insurer for the group member firms [1983, 1984]. (The last of these articles was published in Aoki's *The Economic Analysis of the Japanese Firm* [1984b].) Second, Nakatani contends that the ongoing main bank relationship, an implicit long-term contract, provides a continuous signal of the creditworthiness of the client firm to banks and financial institutions outside the group. Nakatani's overall approach emphasizes the stabilizing effect of the main bank on the long-term performance of the firm. From this starting point a number of hypotheses have been proposed by economists who have sought to elaborate on this approach, principally by focusing on a model describing the efficiency of capital in the main bank relationship and its benefits to the firm.

Informational Properties of the Main Bank Relationship

Some economists [Sheard, 1989, 1991; Aoki 1990] have stressed the main bank's monitoring role, particularly in light of its shareholding in its client firm, suggesting that the relationship represents a form of corporate governance in which the bank acts as the delegated monitor for the group's cross-shareholding member firms. Aoki [1994] parses monitoring into three conceptual stages: *ex ante*, the evaluation of potential new projects of the client firm; *interim*, the ongoing monitoring of the performance of the firm; and *ex post*, the exercise of control over firms in financial distress. What the Aoki model of stylized facts does not consider is that inter-bank competitiveness subverts every stage of the monitoring process. As we will see from the evidence in Chapter 6, non-main banks are only too eager to lend to a client for new *ex ante* projects, thereby gaining a foothold to increase their position in the lending hierarchy, if not displace the main bank. *Interim* monitoring, chiefly done by the bank team, relates more to the sales function of the team as it competes with the teams of other banks, again not an exclusive role of the main bank, but rather one method used by the bank as it vies against a whole hierarchy of rival banks. Finally, *ex post* monitoring efforts by banks are all too often the means for the bank to hasten its own strategic retreat when the client firm is in financial crisis, if possible, in advance of the other competing banks within the lending hierarchy.

In Sheard's [1986, 1989, 1994a, 1994b, 1994d] expansion on Nakatani's thesis, he argues that the main banks are more efficient at gathering information and therefore are able to effect more efficient solutions. This view derives much of its theoretical foundation from Diamond's discussion of information asymmetries and the costs of delegated monitoring in "Financial Intermediation and Delegated Monitoring" [1984] where he asserts that monitoring delegated to a bank as a financial intermediary allows better contracts and Pareto-superior allocations of resources. Sheard [1989, 1994d], in his application of Diamond, relies heavily on anecdotal material from the business press on Japan, citing news stories of the main bank's rescue role in times of financial distress for his evidence. (See Chapter 6 for a discussion on the reliability and use of such "news" stories.) For additional support he points to the dispatch of bank employees on temporary assignments to the client firm and the role of the main bank in negotiating with other creditors for more lenient terms for the client firm.

In our view, *ex post* monitoring, as economists label these work-out efforts, belies the reality that the so-called "rescue" for most firms is the seizure of its collateral and an imposed acquisition by a firm favored by the main bank. The bank is placed in a moral hazard position *vis-à-vis* not only its fellow shareholders but fellow creditors as well. Furthermore, this potential conflict is readily apparent to the other members of the cross-shareholding group who will have observed that the bank's interests as a creditor are not necessarily aligned with its interests as an investor. When those two interests clash, the significance of the bank's role as shareholder will yield to its overriding concern as creditor. Indeed, our evidence shows that the monitoring role, such as it is, places the main bank in the best position to make first claims upon a firm's assets to the detriment of the other principals (i.e. shareholders), or even the firm's other creditors. As chief reorganizer and receiver of the firm in any reorganization plan, the main bank is able to structure the workout to its own optimum advantage, whether it is through dissolution of the firm, the bank's seizing of collateral, or the continued infusion of cash and easing of credit terms with the firm's other banks. The so-called main bank rescue function has come to be more often honored in its breach, rescue of the bank's interests often taking precedence over rescue of the firm itself [author's interviews].

Main Bank as Firm Governor

Following Sheard and Aoki, some agency theory proponents have attempted to show that there is a statistical correlation between firm performance, as measured by positive stock price changes, and the appointment of outside directors who were former bank employees to the firm's board [Kaplan and Minton, 1994; Kang and Shivda-sani, 1995], suggesting that this is a form of corporate governance by the firm's main bank by which the turnover of top executives leads to improved firm performance. The Kaplan–Minton study suffers from a number of errors, however, the first being selection bias. The study is limited to 119 Japanese companies drawn from the *Fortune International 500*, a list that includes the most notoriously poor performers in such sunset industries as steel, shipping, and ship-building.[7] Secondly, the Kaplan–Minton study was confined to a period of a rising bull market in stocks, from 1980 to 1988, when even relatively poorly performing firms were showing improved stock prices in a rapidly expanding economy. Kang and Shivdasani do better in their study, taking great pains to eliminate selection bias, distinguishing between routine and non-routine turnovers of key executives, and employing a larger selection of companies, during the period 1985 to 1990, a period of first rising, then falling stock markets. Of the 270 non-financial firms selected by them from the Moody's International Manual, in only fourteen firms did they find a correlation between outside appointments to the board and the non-routine turnover of the company's president; however, they still carefully disclaimed a causal relationship in this statistical correlation. In only two of those fourteen cases were the outside appointees to the firm's board former bankers. The Kang–Shivdasani study concludes that "the presence of outside directors on the board has no effect on the turnover likelihood. . . . [O]utside succession in Japan appears unrelated to whether departure of the outgoing president was forced. . . . [F]irms belonging to a *keiretsu* [*sic, kigyo shudan*] experience a lower likelihood of succession." Neither set of authors considers or even speculates as to any possible alternative causes for the statistical correlations their methodologies yield.

---

[7] Sheard [1994b] provides another example of selection bias in his "Selected Japanese Corporations and Their Top Shareholders," which is based on an analysis of only five companies, among them a housing finance company, a construction company, and Mazda Motors. All three firms were in financial distress at the time of Sheard's article and long before, and one, a financial firm, is itself affiliated with other financial firms (see fn.2 in Chapter 3 for an explanation). Under such circumstances it was only to be expected that there would be a preponderance of financial institutions among their top shareholders.

By contrast, studies by scholars in Japan generally use non-financial firms listed on the First and Second Sections of the Tokyo Stock Exchange. For example, the Omura survey studied the responses from some 351 firms of the 1501 non-financial firms listed on the TSE. These firms were classified according to their relative financial strengths: by size of capital; efficiency of capital; capital/assets ratio; growth in capital; concentration of ownership; and volatility of stock price. They were then further divided by industry. The Fuji Sogo Kenkyujo study analyzed responses of 1,175 non-financial firms, including 329 from the First Section, 161 in the Second Section, 114 OTC-traded firms, and 570 privately held firms.

Later, in Chapter 6, we discuss what we discovered to be the primary purpose the banks have for the transfer of retiring personnel to client firms. The banks' motivation is a bottom-line financial consideration, but of an altogether different character from exercising control over the client company. Rather, as will be seen later, the purpose relates to the nature of the Japanese management system itself, and specifically to the traditions of long-term employment. The banks actively seek to place their senior (high-wage) personnel in outside companies in order to be able to retire them early from the bank, thereby cutting payroll costs and enabling the advancement of junior level bank employees.

The Main Bank Relationship and the Efficiency of Corporate Finance

Also building on the theories of Nakatani and Diamond, Hoshi *et al.* [1990a, 1990b, 1991] used a statistical sample of 125 firms during the period 1977–82, comparing *kigyo shudan* member firms (45) with "independent" firms (80). It was presumed that the former had close banking ties whereas the latter did not. Hoshi *et al.* then found that the capital investment behavior of the independent firms exhibited a strong sensitivity to the firm's cash flow in comparison to group member firms, and, on that basis, he imputed agency cost benefits to group firms. It should be pointed out, however, that the premise of the selection of the statistical base was severely flawed since non-group firms usually have as close relationships with their main banks as do the *kigyo* group member firms. Although the determining factor in terms of capital expenditure may have related to group membership, the capital efficiencies of main bank monitoring could not have been the decisive factor because it was present to the same degree in both group and independent firms.

R. Okazaki and Horiuchi [1992] directly rebut Hoshi in their study of 38 large electrical equipment manufacturing firms listed in the First Section of the Tokyo Stock Exchange. They utilized a regression analysis of the ratios following three variables—main bank loans, shares held by main bank, and the appointment of former bankers as directors of the client firm—over a period from 1972 through 1988. They found no meaningful distinction in client benefits between *kigyo shudan* firms and non-group firms resulting from the main bank relationship.

The Main Bank Relationship: A Research Agenda

The purported benefits of the main bank relationship to the firm and society have generally been classified in the following three areas: (1) efficiencies of capital derived from the delegated cost of monitoring, the so-called signal function; (2) main bank assistance to firms in financial distress, the so-called rescue function; (3) the main bank role in corporate governance. From the emergence of such analysis, however, the credibility of this hypothesis was questioned by scholars in Japan studying the main bank system. In particular, they questioned the existence of such benefits, the efficacy of the relationship, and the actual role of the group's main bank in risk-sharing, and at least one scholar has even questioned the existence of the main bank itself [Miwa, 1985, 1991].

Agency theorists have emphasized the role of the main bank in "rescuing" companies in financial distress [Sheard, 1989, 1994d], and have asserted that through reciprocal monitoring among members, chiefly by the main bank, there is a reduction of agency costs [Hoshi et al., 1990a, 1990b]. Testing the concept of banks as corporate monitors, some researchers suggested a statistical correlation between firm performance as measured by stock prices and the appointment of former bankers as outside directors to the cross-shareholding firm's board [Kaplan and Minton, 1994] while other researchers [Kang and Shivdasani, 1995] found no such correlation. Still others have challenged these assumptions, calling into question the actual role of the group's main bank in risk-sharing [Horiuchi and Fukuda, 1987; Horiuchi et al., 1988].

Agency economists have placed heavy emphasis upon the information-gathering role of the industrial group's main bank in defining its role. Aoki [1994] focuses upon main bank monitoring and corporate governance; Sheard [1989, 1994a, 1994c, 1994d] upon bank team monitoring, the transfer of bank executives to client firms in financial distress, and purported main bank rescue; and Hoshi et al. [1990a, 1990b] upon lower agency costs by means of the so-called "signal function" which presumably results in efficiencies of corporate finance to the firm. Although these assumptions have been challenged in a number of Japanese studies, for example, those of Horiuchi, R. Okazaki (R. Oba), and Miwa, these studies, however, have been seldom acknowledged, let alone responded to, by agency theorists.

Various series of analytical articles by Horiuchi, Horiuchi and Fukuda, Horiuchi *et al.*, Oba and Horiuchi, and R. Okazaki and Horiuchi have raised questions about the Nakatani and Hoshi view and the efficacy of the main bank relationship, which are also questioned by our research data and the data of the Fuji Research and Omura studies. These last two studies, which reported on the main bank from the perspective of the client firm, revealed that corporate executives generally see the main bank relationship as lacking the benefits it purportedly accords the firm. This view is shared by banker practitioners in our data, and as we will see in greater detail in Chapters 6 and 7, these bankers also dismiss ideas of such benefits to the firm. Yet both the Fuji and the Omura data and our own qualitative data from banker practitioners overwhelmingly show that the main bank relationship exists, is stable and is part and parcel of some very traditional expectations coming from traditional ideas of relationships. Furthermore, although the benefits of the relationship may be doubtful to the client, the bankers believe the relationship is quite beneficial to the profitability of the bank.

Although many economists have analyzed different details and presumed attributes of the main bank system, extrapolating those pieces into theories of the whole, principally agency theory, our research revealed contradictions of fact underpinning these theories. We set about in Chapters 6 and 7 to deal with these conflicts. Our research agenda had presented us with two critical tasks: first, the need to test the "stylized facts" which were used in constructing agency models. This included testing the following propositions: Do banks monitor for corporate governance? Do they send a signal to other creditors? to other investors? Is the correct signal always sent? Do they really "rescue" firms in financial distress? If so, under what circumstances? Are agency costs lower for group firms when compared to non-group member firms? If not, then for what purpose do main banks "monitor"? For what purpose do banks transfer their retired bank executives to client firms? If bank–client relationships in Japan are fixed according to principles of governance and are by nature long-term, why then are banks so highly competitive? What are the benefits of the relationship to the bank?

Second, in agency theories the main bank is a black box, its character and role deduced chiefly from the perceived effects of its actions. The next task was to uncloak that black box and scrutinize the banking system itself: What are the forces that drive competition among banks? Is the competitive pressure among banks undervalued by agency theorists? Does the main bank system even exist?

Chapters 6 and 7 examine all of the issues raised above, revealing the many ways banks compete with each other and the nontransparent methods by which they are rewarded through the main bank relationship.

6 The Main Bank Relationship: *Tatemae* or *Honne*, "Stylized Facts" or Real Facts?

The original objective of the field research was to produce a fine-grained study [Lawler, 1985] of Japanese banking practices as they related to the main bank system and the role of the main bank team in particular. As the research progressed, however, various sub-issues began to acquire greater importance, particularly in light of an increasingly obvious dissonance between Western and Japanese theorists regarding Japanese governance structures. A new and unavoidable objective became evident, to test some of these hypotheses against the research data being gathered. The selection of methodological approach, in particular, was critical because it appeared that many of the conclusions propounded by Western theorists may well have been the result of inadequacies in their research methodologies.

Those who do fieldwork in Japan sooner or later come to know the difference between *tatemae* and *honne*. *Tatemae*, translated literally, means "outer façade" and is always contrasted with *honne* or "the real story." *Tatemae* represents the image a company or group would like to project of itself, particularly in order to conform with the commonly accepted cultural norms of Japanese society. By its very nature, however, *tatemae* eschews actual fact, substituting socially acceptable approximations adapted to fit what is expected. What every Japanese (and every researcher) seeks out, of course, is *honne*, the real truth. Most often that is only revealed after relationships (and therefore access) have achieved a familiar level. As an outsider, the researcher first must confront the ingrained inclination of respondents not to depart from the carefully cultivated image or story.

Tatemae offers a pointed parallel to the "stylized facts" of the economists. A characteristic of agency theory models discussed in

Chapter 5 is their presumption of so-called "stylized facts," such as the Japanese main bank monitoring function, the main bank rescue function, or the main bank control of client firms through equity ownership. As these "facts" were tested in our study, their accuracy became increasingly suspect, not only because of the frequency and regularity with which the cases mentioned by Western economists were recited in my initial interviews, but also because exactly the same examples were constantly cited, even the examples of rather ancient vintage, dating back to the 1970s. In these interviews respondents were at a loss when asked to offer examples from first-hand knowledge, or, for that matter, even different, or more recent examples. Furthermore, the most frequently cited examples, which included Ataka & Co., Mazda Motors, and Asahi Breweries, centered upon Sumitomo Bank's reliability as a rescue partner and were frequently impeached by the very same respondents upon further questioning! Not only does it appear that the corporate communications department of Sumitomo Bank has been quite efficient at disseminating such favorable self-serving lore, such stories continue with a new life of their own as part of the *tatemae* touting the rescue and reorganization prowess of the entire banking industry. I later found out that the heads of the communication departments of banks hold industry-wide monthly meetings together, as do the heads of other bank departments, to discuss common interests and objectives, if not strategies. The anti-trust implications of these practices do not seem to be a factor that Japanese bankers need contend with.

The first part of this chapter discusses the major reasons banks seek out and compete for main bank status and the significance of the profitability motive for main banks and for second and third lending banks. The second part details some of the key components of relationship banking as seen from the banking side.

THE MAIN BANK RELATIONSHIP AND SUTTON'S LAW: THE PROFITABILITY MOTIVE

In the course of attempting to define the bank's role within the Japanese industrial group relationship, it became immediately apparent during the preliminary interviews with bankers that they

viewed the main bank relationship quite differently from the prevailing academic interpretation, which many bankers thought was in
fact a rather naive view of main bank practices. To my first general
question "Why the main bank relationship?" I frequently received
what could be called the Willie Sutton response. When that infa-
mous American bank robber of the 1940s and 1950s was asked by a
reporter why he robbed banks, Sutton replied: "That's where the
money is!"

In general, the literature to date has tended to emphasize the
benefits of the main bank relationship to the corporate enterprise or
to the economic development of society, particularly in times of
scarcity of capital. Often treating the bank as a "black box," these
studies, cited in earlier chapters, focus upon the role of the main
bank within the industrial group, in cross-shareholding arrangements with its client firms, monitoring in corporate governance,
while other studies focus upon the main bank's purported role as
lender of last resort, the so-called rescue function. Only a few
scholars have noted in passing the pecuniary forces central to main
bank strategy and organization. For example, the Horiuchi–Packer–
Fukuda hypothesis [1988], which focused on information asymmetries, took for granted that banks continue their relationship with
their client firms for only as long as the knowledge they gain is
profitable and exceeds the cost of their risk in supporting the firm.
Sheard [1991] conceded that the main bank would be unlikely to
shoulder the costs of a corporate rescue, either in terms of admin-
istration or increased risk-bearing, without the expectation of being
able to maintain close transactional ties with the firm in the future.

My research sought to test the assumptions of these studies
regarding the main bank's relationship with its client firms. This
was not an easy task since there is no universally agreed-upon
definition of what constitutes a firm's "main bank," either among
scholars or, for that matter, among bankers themselves. Therefore,
among the questions bankers were asked was what being the main
bank meant. What direct rewards were sought by the banks? How
were the bank's needs served by being a main bank? Their answers
shed light on some of the hitherto under-reported aspects of the
main bank relationship, namely, what the areas of real profitability
are for the banks, why second and third banks in the lending
hierarchy can expect the same kind of profitability, though to a

lesser degree, and what the main bank relationship involves for the banks.

Our research found that by their own accounts bankers overwhelmingly regard the main bank relationship as the source of their greatest profitability. Whereas in earlier years banks had prioritized increasing the volume of lending as their chief strategy, in the postwar regulatory regime of fixed interest rates lending profits were all but guaranteed. However, profitability had become a key concern by the early 1990s. Pressure on banks to improve profitability had escalated in the face of interest rate deregulation and narrowing spreads on lending, the Bank for International Settlements (BIS) capital/assets ratio requirements, and the rapidly deteriorating quality of bank assets which resulted from underperforming real-estate-related loans. By common definition, main bank status signifies that the bank is the largest lender to the client corporation among all of the banks with which the company conducts its banking business. This status confers major rewards on the bank way beyond the current rewards of corporate lending. These rewards include receiving the main depository accounts of the firm, non-interest-bearing compensating balance accounts (formerly called *ryodate* accounts), low-interest time deposit accounts, and a disproportionately large share of the client's commission and fee-based business. These rewards have gained even greater importance since the liberalization of Japanese financial markets which has led to narrow lending margins and diminished profits from large corporate lending.

Depository and Compensating Balance Accounts

From the bank's viewpoint, the [main bank] relationship is a major source of profit. Because of interest rates and the need to keep a compensating balance, clients must keep money in their transaction account, and not a small amount. These accounts are non-interest-bearing . . . [or low-interest-bearing].[8]

---

[8] Respondent #1 at Bank I: An officer of a long-term credit bank.

The true importance of depository and compensating balance accounts is understood only when it is also understood that these accounts reflect not only deposit taking but the transaction-fee generating aspects of a large-sized firm's relationship with several banks. It is also likely that a medium-sized business would have more than one current deposit account—at least one for operational expenses and others for large-scale expenses and purchases. A very small company usually will have only one account, and the bank which has the company's current deposit account will be considered by that company to be its main bank.[9]

Respondents typically emphasized the connection between profitability and depository accounts, and often reported as least profitable the lending side of the business, i.e., return on assets (ROA).

Respondent: The main bank is usually in the most profitable position because it gets the largest share of a company's deposits as well as [the largest share] of its other profitable business, such as foreign exchange.

Question: Then the unprofitable parts . . .

Respondent: are the loans, because what we are talking about is return on assets, right? We are talking about the management of banks under the new BIS regulations.[10]

Lending is regarded as a "loss leader" in the portfolio of financial services provided by the main bank. The lower cost of loans is rationalized not by their lower risk but by their use as a competitive vehicle in merchandising more profitable banking services to the client.

Fee-based and Commission Banking

With lending diminished in profitability, banks have increasingly turned to fee-based banking, which requires no commitment of

---

[9] Respondent #1 at Bank D: An officer of a top six city bank.
[10] Respondent #2 formerly of Bank H: A former officer of a long-term credit bank.

funds. Fee-based banking has expanded enormously in recent years and is seen by most Japanese bankers as one of the best ways to observe the BIS regulations because there are no assets behind the transaction.[11] Fee-based products include foreign exchange transactions, letters of credit, and exchanging foreign currency.[12]

When extending credit, the bank considers whether the loan transaction will lead to expanding the amount of the company's deposits in the bank, or its fee services, or to increasing employee salary deposits. If a company seeks to increase its borrowing from other banks, then its main bank will often apply pressure upon the company for an increase also and to receive a greater share of the company's other business. The bank typically expects an increased share of the company's loans, foreign exchange, transfer payments to public utilities, and other fee-based services. However, severe competition means each bank will try to get as much as possible, and as a result, the main bank can never get it all. Although the main bank of a company in its *kigyo shudan* will almost never change, it is possible through competition to get independent companies to change their main bank, or at least change the second and third position banks.[13]

Employee Accounts

The personal accounts of employees of client firms represent one of the greatest rewards to the main bank in the relationship. Much of the ensuing relationship between bank and firm is predicated on these accounts. Companies will "request" all of their personnel to open accounts at the main bank for the direct deposit of their salary. Furthermore, identification of the bank with the company also encourages employees to conduct their personal business with the bank. How successfully a bank wins over this captive client base depends, at least in part, on how strong a group consciousness exists at the company.

---

[11] Respondent #1 at Bank C: An officer of a top six city bank.
[12] Respondent #1 at Bank C: An officer of a top six city bank.
[13] Respondent #1 at Bank D: An officer of a top six city bank.

The percentage of employees [who comply] often depends on the size of the company. Usually, in smaller and medium-sized companies there is more of a family type of atmosphere, *ie ishiki*—family consciousness—among all the people at the company, its managers and employees, particularly if the branches of the bank are convenient to their own households. The level of compliance relates to the level of *ie* consciousness.[14]

Employees' personal accounts also become an important source of cheap funds by which the bank, through intermediation, can recycle employee savings back to the client company. In exchange for these benefits, the bank provides the corporation with a credit safety net and main bank services.

Group member companies usually get better credit terms. They also don't have to put up as large a compensating deposit. But, in return, of course, the bank expects to receive more of the transactions from a group company—as their main bank. For example, all the employees of the core Mitsui group companies put their deposits in the Sakura Bank. . . . It's direct deposit now. Ten or fifteen years ago it was given out as cash. But for large companies now it's almost all direct deposit and they use it for other services as well. All the employees put all of their deposits into the Sakura Bank, and if they need a housing loan they receive priority at the Sakura Bank. It's a captive market.[15]

Employee accounts generally bring other benefits. A large base of employee accounts means a significant amount of business for the bank in the retail sector, normally a high-profit-margin area. The bank is rewarded with a large volume of consumer transactions in the form of electronic transfers, consumer lending, personal lending, credit card, mortgages, etc.

The main bank relationship provides a safety net for its companies. A very large bank has a very large commitment to its

---

[14] Respondent #1 at Bank D: An officer of a top six city bank.
[15] Respondent #1: President of bank services organization.

customer, like Mitsubishi Bank to Mitsubishi Corporation. When things get rough, the Mitsubishi Corporation can always go back to the bank, or to Meiji Life, which is in the same group. Having a main bank behind it lowers the risk for the company, and for the bank it means a very large percentage of all types of transactions of the client are concentrated in the bank. Considering all the Mitsubishi companies together, they have hundreds of thousands of employees with accounts in the bank. Whenever an individual has to make a transfer, he has to pay ¥300–400, and that represents a very large amount of revenue for Mitsubishi Bank. ¥300–400 for an electronic transfer—that's really exorbitant compared to the cost of [personal] checks in the U.S.[16]

As the emphasis on profits increases, it is not surprising that the extent of the main bank's efforts to maintain its relationship with the client firm is often directly proportional to the size of the captive employee base. The focus has shifted away from volume corporate lending and towards emphasizing business relationships with retail customers.

What we do is no different from any other bank. We are aiming to use the main bank position not only for firms, but also for individuals and households, providing housing loans, credit cards, other settlement services, such as utilities, card loans, everything. By their concentrating those transactions in us, we are giving them some benefits, such as lowering some interest rates on loans. Many other city banks are doing the same thing.[17]

Of course, having a profitable relationship depends not only on the company but also on having a banking relationship with that company's employees. So, taking all those factors into account, we think that it's profitable but sometimes difficult to analyze those type of transactions.[18]

---

[16] Respondent #1: President of bank services organization.
[17] Respondent #1 at Bank B: Senior officer of a top six city bank.
[18] Respondent #1 at Bank B: Senior officer of a top six city bank.

Competition for Profits Among the Lead "Main" Banks

Although the highly-coveted status of the main bank is hard to displace, the status of second or third bank also provides desirable opportunities to receive substantial business, and these positions are much sought after by competing lending banks. These second and third "main" banks are often significantly involved in the day-to-day financial dealings of client firms.

A typical large company may do business with some 20 to 30 banks but use only three to five of the lead banks for most, if not all, of its fee-based transactions, such as foreign exchange, swap transactions, underwriting, or leasing by the bank's affiliated securities and leasing affiliates or overseas subsidiaries. Although the top five banks may supply less than 50% of their client's borrowing needs, they will receive nearly 100% of its fee-based business. The opportunity for banks below the top five to acquire profitable business with the client outside of lending has become quite remote, principally because corporations themselves are attempting to rationalize their relations. Therefore, a bank which has an unprofitable relationship with a company will first attempt to improve its fee-based business with the client before it seeks to recall its loan.[19]

The distribution of expected fee-based transactions from the client corporation to its top five lending banks is not strictly based on the bank's percentage of the client's loans. A company usually concentrates most of its fee-based business in its main bank, and next in its second and third lenders. The following is a case in point offered by an officer of the second lead bank of a very large, established company. Dai-Ichi Kangyo is the company's main bank. Respondent's bank is in second position. The company has six major banks: DKB, respondent's bank, IBJ, Mitsubishi, and Fuji, and one other. Of those, five account for 50% of the company's borrowing. DKB has 16% or 17%, respondent's bank has about 8%. Together DKB and respondent's bank receive in the range of 40–50% of the company's fee-based business; the remaining 60% is divided among the other four banks. In this case, the main bank will receive more

---

[19] Respondent #1 at Bank B: Senior officer of a top six city bank.

than twice its loan percentage in fee-based business, and, by supplying 50% of the company's loans, the top six banks receive 100% of the fee-based business.

> We want to be in the stable number two position, but the other banks also are competing for that spot. If we are number two we will always be the co-lead manager on bond issues. Our bank is not a member of any *kigyo shudan*, but we are in a good position with our clients. If a company borrows from ten banks, number one is their main bank, but we usually are the second, third, or fourth bank. That puts us in a good position to promote a lot of business with that client. If we were very low [in the hierarchy], then we would not have the opportunity to do foreign exchange business for that client. But if we are positioned very well, then we can get that type of business. We would try to be promoted from fourth to third, or third to second position.[20]

Bankers at some leading institutions see the decrease in the main bank's lending to their clients as an opportunity to increase business through bank-facilitated access to the money market. They view Japan as a whole as still achieving so-called over-saving, despite the current tight money economy, and therefore still having plenty of funds. While a number of large corporations are claiming that some of the major city banks are limiting their lending volume because of the BIS regulations, these bankers deny any such problems and point to increased bank-assisted financing through the straight bond market, both domestically and internationally by the bank's over-seas subsidiaries,[21] and since 1994 by domestic bank-owned securities underwriting subsidiaries.

Bankers acknowledge that a particular bank's capabilities and expertise to meet a company's need may be determinative in the placement of its fee-based business, outweighing the influence of the percentage of lending supplied by its lead banks. The bank that can offer the most types of services clearly has an advantage. Despite ranking order, the type of transaction a company is seeking will

---

[20] Respondent #1 at Bank I: An officer of a long-term credit bank.
[21] Respondent #1 at Bank A: An officer of a top six city bank.

usually decide which bank gets that portion of its business. As in the case of bond market underwriting, a company will tend to go to the bank which specializes in the desired financial service. Therefore, a company's collateral banking business is not all destined for its top banks in strict hierarchical order. The arrangement is often much looser and dependent on the needs of each company and the capabilities of each bank.

> The percentage of transactions is just one criterion. Decisions are not based solely on the amount of lending. When it comes to Eurobond issues, for example, some other banks might not have our capabilities. It depends upon each company and each bank, and the type of transactions. It is not fixed. There is a loose relation but it's not well defined.[22]

Although the exact percentage of distribution of each fee-based service is not precisely defined and is highly dependent upon the individual capabilities of each bank, the hierarchy among the lending institutions is strictly observed by the firm, and a variety of devices are employed by the client corporation to preserve the relative standing overall among the lending institutions. There is a tacit understanding that, no matter what, the corporation will make sure that its main bank comes out on top at the end of the fiscal year. This is true even when only a single percent of lending separates the first and second banks. That additional 1% is almost impossible to overcome until the top management decides to change their policy as to which is their main bank.[23]

A corporation will go to great lengths to maintain the relative ranking of its lenders and to protect its relationship to that bank. This includes the disguising of transactions and borrowing patterns so that the firm's financial statement reflects the established hierarchy. Foreign-owned banks, which lack the established long-term client relationships of Japanese banks, are customarily excluded from the role of main bank. However, even loans from foreign banks and from domestic insurance companies that are not part of

---

[22] Respondent #1 at Bank H: An officer of a long-term credit bank.
[23] Respondent #2 formerly of Bank H: A former officer of a long-term credit bank.

the company's industrial group are managed in such a way as to prevent public disclosure. For example, such loans are timed to terminate before the end of the fiscal period so that they will go unreported in the firm's annual statement.

The following is the explanation of a Japanese officer of a foreign-owned bank. This bank is often not listed among the lead lending institutions of any major company, yet it plays an important role in maintaining the hierarchical equilibrium even though, unacknowledged and anonymous, it occupies no position in the hierarchy.

The rationing of collateral business among Japanese banks is quite important. It is part of a mutual understanding whenever we, or another foreign-owned bank, make a loan. Financial closings are usually September or March. Normally, Japanese companies don't want us to continue a loan over the closing of the period, from September into October. That way their balance sheets don't indicate any loans from us.

The companies don't want it to appear that they have any loans from our bank because they must report to the stock exchange [on the public record] how much they owe to each bank. It's less of a consideration that we're not a Japanese bank. Their most important concern is to prioritize [the reported ranking] of the levels of lending among the banks, which banks will be second and third in their lending and so on.

In fact, since we don't have a huge depository base, we always try to be an arranger rather than a lender. However, when we arrange a private placement with an insurance company, the same issue of ranking arises. For example, a company's main life insurance company may be Nippon Life Insurance, then Meiji, or Sumitomo, or some other. If we try to intermediate a loan for the company with Dai-Ichi Life Insurance, for example, the company won't want Dai-Ichi Life to be disclosed on their financial statement. Why? It will destroy the order of the relationship.[24]

---

[24] Respondent #1 at Bank P: An officer of a foreign-owned bank, formerly an officer of a top six bank.

COMPONENTS OF THE BANK–CLIENT RELATIONSHIP

The Nature of Main Bank Relationships

Going beyond the most narrow definition of the "main bank" as having the lead share in lending, we find that a firm's second and third lending banks, sometimes referred to as the "second and third main banks," also play a significant role as "main bank" to the client. Although the main bank is likely to be the largest shareholder among the banks lending to the client firm, by law each bank is restricted to a maximum 5% stake in the client corporation. However, the second and third lending banks are usually significant shareholders as well, often approaching and sometimes even equaling the main bank's shareholding in the client. These top three or four lenders comprise the banks with which the client maintains "relationship banking."

If one were to ask twelve bankers for a definition of "relationship banking" or "main bank," you would likely receive a dozen differing responses. The terms themselves, as they are used in Japan, are rather ambiguous—a common characteristic of the language. Since the terms are used as English phrases and written phonetically in *katakana* (syllabic alphabet used chiefly for the transliteration of foreign words and concepts), they mask, in fact, very custom-bound processes.

Bankers' descriptions of relationship banking in Japan generally reflected four different definitions having in common some expression of a relational system of designated rewards and protection based on traditions of insider–outsider status:

(a) As an historical development of the immediate postwar reconstruction period arising out of the need to ration capital for economic development;

(b) As the successor to the prewar *zaibatsu* bank, the group bank today in the *kigyo shudan*;

(c) As a manifestation of traditional hierarchical and communal relationships with strong components of *giri* (obligations), *onjoshugi* (paternalism), and *ie ishiki* (family consciousness); and

(d) The functional view which sees the principal differentiation as being between relationship banking versus *ad hoc* deal banking.

We will now review these in turn, as they were described by the bankers themselves.

(a) The Historical View: Government Economic Development Policy

The historical explanation generally given by the bankers ascribes the origins of relationship banking to the post-World War II era.[25] At that time domestic funds were in extremely short supply, and the capital market was in its infancy. Most companies were solely dependent upon bank lending for funding. Due to the shortage of funds, no company could rely on a single bank but had to contract with as many banks as possible. Thus it became common for a large corporation to deal with as many as 20 or 30 banks. In addition, as part of its economic policy, the government designated certain industries—steel, coal mining, shipbuilding—as having first priority to bank funds, and it established the three long-term credit banks to supply them with funds. The seven existing trust banks were also permitted to invest funds. The mission of the city banks at that time was to supply short-term working capital to industry as a whole.[26]

Since 1951 the mechanism that has continued to be used by the government to designate specific industries for development funds is the government-owned Japan Development Bank (JDB), whose main source of funds are from deposits collected through the Japanese postal savings system. The city and long-term credit banks, such as IBJ, are eager to participate, leading to the so-called "cowbell effect" in which commercial banks follow the "cowbell" call of the JDB in making loans. Because the JDB, as a government-owned institution, can be the largest lender but not take deposits nor serve as a main bank, the commercial banks gain the opportunity to reap main bank profits from employee and depository accounts with a lesser commitment of their own funds.[27]

---

[25] This view, standard during the earliest sets of interviews, has now been replaced by the new "historiography" described in Chapter 5, according to which the main bank system is said to have originated during the wartime period.

[26] Respondents #1 and #2 at Bank A: Officers of a top six city bank.

[27] Respondent #1 at Bank O: Senior officer of a government-owned bank.

(b) The Successor to the Zaibatsu *Bank View*

The group bank in the *kigyo shudan* is often labeled the successor to the prewar *zaibatsu* bank. After World War II the *zaibatsu* holding companies were dissolved, and much of their shares were suddenly on the market being traded by so-called hot money. As a consequence, many of these companies sought to establish a steady relationship with a bank to serve as their major lender and stable shareholder. This relationship followed the pattern of the group bank of the *zaibatsu*, in which a bank like Sumitomo or Mitsubishi prioritized funds to its group member companies, just as the main bank does today in the *kigyo shudan*.[28] The notable exception to this pattern would appear to be the group bank of the Mitsui group. The statistical lending data on the Sakura Bank, the Mitsui group bank, would seem to suggest, at least superficially, that the bank has relatively weaker ties as reflected in its reduced lending to group member corporations which are less than the banks of other *kigyo shudan*. However, this can be attributed to a lack of funding capacity resulting from the particular historical circumstances of the Mitsui Bank's postwar dissolution.

(c) The Cultural View: Traditional Hierarchical and Communal Relations

The social values implicit in traditional hierarchical and communal relationships, such as *giri* (obligation), *onjoshugi* (paternalism), and *ie ishiki* (family consciousness) were often mentioned by older bankers. A retired senior city bank official described the pervasiveness of a sense of obligation felt by a company towards its main bank even when the company was not in need of borrowing money. "Companies will continue to maintain a *ryodate* [compensating balance] to keep their line of credit and to keep up good relations with the bank out of a sense of *giri ninjo*" (obligation). As an officer of a trust bank explained, the absence of *giri* indicates, in a sense, the absence of a relationship.[29]

---

[28] Respondents #1 and #2 at Bank A: Officers of a top six city bank.
[29] Respondent #1 at Bank N: An officer of a trust bank.

The banks, for their part, maintain an advisory and monitoring role, asking for and studying the company's data so that they know everything about the company. This is done with a sense of *onjo* (paternalism) which ensures that "the company will be faithful to the bank." In describing this relationship senior bankers used the familial term *oya-ginko,* parent bank, rather than the relatively recent term "main bank."[30] Intra-groups relations are supported also through the promotion of *ie ishiki*—family consciousness—particularly among employees of the client company who are encouraged to conduct their personal business with the company's main bank.

The present generation of bankers are apt to find the use of such traditional terminology somewhat anachronistic. But as one younger officer conceded: "There may not be much *ninjo* (human kindness) in banking relations these days, but a little *giri* to the bank can go a long way in helping business."[31]

(d) The Functional View

The functional description of relationship banking centers on the role of the "relationship manager." The basic strategy of relationship banking, according to this view, is for the bank to create a one-stop banking center for its corporate clients, a kind of supermart of products and services. Indeed, the banks have developed a multitude of financial products, including currency swaps, interest rate swaps, and more exotic swaps. They have expanded into securitization, developing many investment targets, and also focused on tax-driven transactions, such as equity participation in leveraged leasing, financing, and so on.

This wide range of services makes it impossible for the bank to draw up a single line of menus that will fit every client. The role of the relationship manager is to act like a window through which the corporate client can access and mobilize the bank's resources. It is essential that a relationship manager know something about practically everything, but he does not need to have comprehensive

---

[30] Respondent #1 at Bank G: A retired director of a former specialized city bank.

[31] Respondent #2 at Bank I: An officer of a long-term credit bank.

knowledge about anything. His job is to bring in the right experts from the right departments.

For example, if the client is inquiring about the availability of funds, questions of creditworthiness and pricing are raised. Typically, the relationship manager will talk to bank headquarters, which sets guidelines as to how much of a loan it will be able to extend and on what terms and conditions, that is, pricing. Within those guidelines, the relationship manager will mobilize the resources of the bank. With the investment banking department, he will try to identify interesting projects. Then he will call up other financial engineering departments to see if any cheap and stable financing is available. He may also call up the foreign exchange department to see if they can get a good spot rate for the contract. If a manager's accounts are very important, he may have only one or two clients (and their subsidiaries) to look after because their needs become so extensive.

Relationship managers are typically rotated every two years or three years, at most. They are selected for the position six to eight years after joining the bank, at around age 30. Although that manager's experience at that point is considered relatively scant, he is selected from among the most promising young employees and is supported by seasoned bankers and the senior manager.[32]

The trend towards relationship managers now extends beyond just the large banks, which use special relationship managers for their corporate clients. The practice has been taken up by the smaller city banks as a means to promote more corporate finance and increase their profitability.[33]

Competitive Strategy

In a sense, every bank and every company has a group. Being a member of a group, whether a large *kigyo shudan* or a small regional grouping, will give the bank a competitive advantage over non-

---

[32] Respondent #2 formerly of Bank H: A former officer of a long-term credit bank.
[33] Respondent #2 formerly of Bank H: A former officer of a long-term credit bank.

group financial institutions.[34] Although it is improbable that the main bank will be displaced from its lead position by another bank, it is virtually impossible if the client corporation and its main bank are members of the same *kigyo shudan*.[35] The rare case of a change in lead lending status is usually the result of a temporary increase in lending in some year by the trust bank member of the same group for some capital expenditure, such as a construction project that may be beyond the lending capabilities of the firm's leading main bank.

Nevertheless, it does sometimes happen that a company changes its main bank for good reason. This occurs most typically in a small or medium-sized company. One commonly cited reason is that the company president simply gets angry with the bank.[36] This is a virtually impossible outcome for a large company and its main bank because of the number of temporarily transferred or retired former bank employees at the company. Most typically, it happens when a small company outgrows its current bank, usually a regional bank from which it is said to "graduate." For example, a very small, domestically-oriented company, whose sales have gone from ¥10 million to ¥4.5 billion in just five years, wants to go abroad. Dissatisfied with the limited capabilities of its current bank, the company goes out to find a banker with a more long-term perspective and a bank with extensive international experience. The company has also become large enough so that a major bank will be seriously interested in doing business with it.[37]

Despite the fact that a regional or second-tier regional (former *sogo*) bank might have more branches in a given local area than a large city bank, the city bank nonetheless has a competitive advantage because the interest on its loans is lower and its total amount of funds is larger. And, most important, the larger city bank has available to it much more information and a wider range of business contacts useful to the client company. By contrast, the second-tier

---

[34] Respondent #2 at Bank O: Senior officer of a government-owned bank.
[35] Respondent #1 at Bank P: An officer of a foreign-owned bank, formerly an officer of a top six bank.
[36] Respondent #1 at Bank B: Senior officer of a top six city bank.
[37] Respondent #2 formerly of Bank H: A former officer of a long-term credit bank.

regional banks do their business in local areas because they take higher risks and have easier credit standards.[38]

When banks compete against each other for the same client, each bank tries to ensure that it gets at least the full share to which it is entitled of the company's business. So if a company wants to increase its borrowing from one of its lending banks, that bank will expect the company to increase its ancillary business with the bank proportionately, or even more. This business includes several groups of services: foreign exchange, transfer payments to public utilities, and other fee-based services. With each bank striving to get as much as possible, the main bank never gets 100%.[39]

The Kansai Style of Competition

Some of the banks, notably those which were historically based in the Kansai (Osaka) region, have developed a reputation for an innovative and aggressive style in pursuing relations with clients and potential clients that goes well beyond the usual excesses of the "bubble period." The key elements to their approach include a willingness to skirt around customary guidelines and to employ adventurous tactics described by the bankers themselves as "hara-kiri." The banks are also noted for their ability to target potential growth companies, regardless of any group affiliations. Once a company is targeted, the bank tries by any and all means to become its main bank.

Traditionally Japanese banks tend to think on a long-term basis when acquiring new customers. A client's initial business is only an opening to the future. To gain that entry, an interloper bank will sometimes employ what they call a hara-kiri strategy to win clients, usually offering up some Euro-issue or other item at a loss to the bank. The bank's act of "hara-kiri" in taking a loss it can otherwise ill afford must be covered up on their books by shadow accounts or other similar tactics.[40]

---

[38] Respondent #1 at Bank D: An officer of a top six city bank.
[39] Respondent #1 at Bank D: An officer of a top six city bank.
[40] Respondent #1 at Bank P: An officer of a foreign-owned bank, formerly an officer of a top six bank.

Officers of Tokyo-based banks often displayed disdain for such aggressive tactics, citing in particular the two leading Kansai banks for their frequent refusal to cooperate with other banks in assisting a mutual client firm, despite press reports to the contrary, thus leaving those client firms in the lurch. One Tokyo banker referred to these two banks as "rivals trying to surpass each other in rudeness." [41]

Responsibilities of the Lead Main Bank: Purported Rescue Function

First among the perceived responsibilities of the main bank, according to the conventional view, is its obligation to provide rescue and a safety net to the client firm in trouble. Although often only informally acknowledged, the responsibilities of the main bank to resolve its client's problems are said to bear the full weight of duty and obligation.

> When a business goes bankrupt here, usually the main bank leads the rescue, or becomes the leader of a settlement, something like a [bankruptcy] trustee in the U.S. I think in the U.S. if there is some problem, the biggest lenders will quickly withdraw, but here in Japan the situation is different in that the main bank has to solve the problems of the business corporation and mitigate the social impact in many other areas. [42]

In actual practice, however, bankers concede that this obligation is generally balanced against considerations of profitability. If a client's circumstances are deemed too bleak or irretrievable, even its main bank will not step forward to mitigate the situation.

> I don't think the banks felt obliged to do that kind of operation, even in the 1950s and 1960s. Banks will act if they believe they can earn profits through the rescue operation and because it will also strengthen their relationship with the customer. If the customer can be bailed out and then prospers, the customer will depend

---

[41] Respondent #2 at Bank B: An officer of a top six city bank.
[42] Respondent #1 at Bank H: An officer at a long-term credit bank.

upon the bank, and the bank can then grant it further loans and take their deposits. But if there is no potential for recovery, then banks will not undertake the rescue operation.[43]

The degree to which the rescue function exists is more a matter of perception on the part of the client than contractual. Bankers report that they are loath to make even an implicit commitment. The actual existence of the rescue function is decided case by case on its merits. Bankers also report that often the most significant factor beyond the particular merits is the "suggestion" by the MoF that the bank support an enterprise or industry whose demise the government deems will have repercussions upon the social and/or strategic economic fabric of the nation. Implicit in the bank's willingness to provide funds to a sunset industry is the understanding that MoF will reward the bank by granting it some concession in another area.

In good times the basic task of the main bank is to meet the needs of that company's development, to help the company raise its annual earnings, develop its resources, expand its transactions, and so on. However, the overriding characteristic that distinguishes the main bank from the second and third banks is that it is by custom the creditor of last resort for the firm in financial distress. The main bank is expected to initiate any rescue plan among the other banks. It is presumed that the main bank's status as the company's largest lender and its access to superior information would normally alert it to problems and enable it to determine whether the company's problems were due to a temporary liquidity crisis or to more fundamental problems of insolvency.

When the company is having difficulty, the main bank's task is to reconstruct, reform, or financially support the company as much as possible to achieve a rescue. The bank will send some of its employees to work within the company. It is quite possible that in the near final stages the task of the main bank will be to ask some member company of its *kigyo shudan* to take over the company or find some other enterprise to merge with the troubled company.[44] The typical response of the other lead banks to a company in trouble

---

[43] Respondent #2 at Bank I: An officer of a long-term credit bank.
[44] Respondent #1 at Bank D: An officer of a top six city bank.

is not to commit more funds. The percentage of loans by the main bank increases as a consequence. If the second, third, and fourth lead banks had provided extremely large loans, the main bank would not be able to take over these liabilities, and a meeting of the bank creditors to resolve the situation would be required.[45]

This problem became particularly acute after the loose monetary conditions of the "bubble economy" of the 1980s. The banks had continually increased their number of customers and expanded their opportunities to make loans. Along with this growth, the traditional bank practice of frequent client interviews and visiting customers became very relaxed; the opportunity for the corporation to give the bank up-to-date information was reduced. In some cases, the bank did not find out about a company's trouble until the very last moment.[46]

The Bank Team: Monitoring or Sales Function?

The primary vehicle for carrying out the main bank relationship is the bank team assigned to large client firms. The team typically consists of a lending officer, foreign exchange officer, and may number four or more officers, depending on the size of the client and the nature of the client's transactional business with the bank. They visit the client's business premises and other points of operation on a daily basis, interacting with the financial officers of the corporation, as well as collecting receipts, advising and consulting on specific issues, and generally acquiring useful information as to current operations and what future plans are under consideration. The team is considered the most effective way of doing business and maintaining the close contact required by the main bank relationship. The second and even the third banks of a major corporation will also assign teams to service a larger client.

The bank team will often visit the various units and locations of the client firm. Frequently, they will also be called upon not only to consult with the financial officers and the accounting department

---

[45] Respondent #1 at Bank D: An officer of a top six city bank.
[46] Respondent #1 at Bank D: An officer of a top six city bank.

there but sometimes to attend to the private banking affairs of the employees.[47] Such attentiveness, however, comes at a price, which is sometimes very high. Banks therefore tend to take a pragmatic approach, estimating profit from overall corporate and employee transactions versus cost. If too much cost is associated with employee services, then the allocation of the time of the banking team is reprioritized to reflect those estimations.[48]

The main bank relationship works quite differently when applied to small and medium-sized businesses than to the major corporations, usually defined as those listed on the Tokyo Stock Exchange. A medium-sized company may have only one person assigned to it at the bank's branch office, and that person may service/monitor as many as ten to twenty, or more, such companies. Small companies receive scarcely any attention. Such an overload of clients means that the banker's primary activity becomes promoting new business among these companies, encouraging them to increase their deposits, persuading them to join the credit loan system, or to join the bank's direct transfer system. At the same time the banker is supposed to inquire about how the client is doing and review its monthly balance, but such attentions can only be cursory at best.[49]

By the early 1980s most banks had abandoned their credit analysis sections. It was quite apparent from the interviews that the bank team's function was not monitoring but rather that of a sales team. Indeed, senior- and middle-level bank management reported that a generation of young bankers recruited during that period received no training in evaluating client creditworthiness and only recently has senior management taken remedial steps to train them belatedly in these skills.[50]

Establishing Main Bank Relationships with New Clients

One major aspect of relationship banking requires the bank to supply its client with useful "information" in the form of contacts

---

[47] Respondent #1: President of bank services organization.
[48] Respondent #1 at Bank C: An officer of a top six city bank.
[49] Respondent #1 at Bank D: An officer of a top six city bank.
[50] Respondent #6 at Bank D. An officer of a top six city bank.

for business deals among its other client firms. By playing the role of matchmaker, and by simultaneously supplying other related consultant services, the main bank (or the second, third, or even fourth main bank) provides its client firm with an opportunity to obtain expert advice, often at no direct cost. At many banks whole departments are set up to advise potential and existing clients, giving out practical advice on how to set up a new subsidiary or other business. Big banks have a decided edge in this kind of competition because they cover a wider area and can provide a wider range of information and introductions than smaller banks.

Medium-sized companies, according to some bankers, tend to consider the ability of the bank to arrange introductions and to provide its "good offices" in promoting business between its clients of paramount importance, even more so than the interest rate on the bank's lending. In the *kigyo shudan* such *eigyo assen* (business assistance) is usually arranged by the group bank, particularly when new co-ventures are in need of financing. Independent companies especially rely upon their main banks to provide contacts for these business introductions.[51]

Such services foster a sense of *giri* in the client, feelings of obligatory indebtedness towards the bank. There will often be no direct fee for the service so that the client is expected to show its gratitude by placing a deposit in a low-interest rate account, or perhaps by offering to improve the bank's position within the ranks of those banks with which the firm does business. Thus a second, third, or fourth main bank can raise its rank among the lenders and even become the lead underwriter or the main bank for a new subsidiary as a reward for its assistance.

Although it is undeniably in the best position, the head company's main bank does not automatically become the main bank for the subsidiaries or the subordinated affiliates of its client firm, even in a *keiretsu*. By providing useful information and expertise for the client's new venture another bank may open window of opportunity for it to become the main bank for the new subsidiary. Generally, a bank's strategy in the case of a large corporation is not to attempt to take away another bank's main client, a difficult and usually

---

[51] Respondent #3 at Bank G: An officer of a former specialized city bank.

fruitless task, but rather to acquire the business of a new subsidiary company just starting out. A bank will use various products and services to build a relationship with a new client, adopting a long-term strategy. Some banks will supply internal strategic advice or provide companies with consulting services, often without fee, until they list their new shares.[52] Similarly, a bank may try to raise its status in the lending hierarchy by providing business introductions which have been targeted through its research on the company's distribution channels.[53]

The main bank does have an inside track on information regarding the development of a new subsidiary or a relationship with another company. Often, the main bank is brought into the expansion process to provide advice about some place to invest, or where to seek information about a new factory. The bank may then act on that information to approach the subsidiary, although the parent company may simply ask its main bank to create a new account for its subsidiary. However, the client may also involve other banks which are not its main bank, if the relationship is a long-term one, often seeking advice from two or three banks in order to get the best information. Thus it is possible for a bank which is not the main bank but is among the top two or three lenders to have access to what is going on in the client firm and become the main bank for the new subsidiary.[54]

Shukko Relations: Trimming Bank Costs, Supplying the Client with Expertise

An established way of providing clients with financial expertise is through the transfer of bank employees. The process of sending out or transferring bank workers to client firms and government agencies, known as *shukko*, may involve junior or senior employees, each for quite different purposes.

---

[52] Respondent #1: Senior consultant of bank services organization.
[53] Respondent #1: Senior consultant of bank services organization.
[54] Respondent #1 at Bank B: Senior officer of a top six city bank.

When a younger bank employee, typically in his 30s or perhaps early 40s, is assigned to a client firm, he is expected to acquire valuable experience in the operations of the firm, while his placement forges ties between the company or government agency and the bank. A bank employee who trains at a government agency, such as the Economic Planning Agency, will typically spend two or three years there before returning to the bank. The age range for such employees can vary from late 20s to late 30s, and such assignments are seen as accomplishing both training and relationship building.

The transfer of a seasoned bank officer, sometimes in his late 40s or more typically 50s, signals a more permanent transfer. He will be sent to a main bank client firm which is in need of an experienced senior financial officer and which has come to rely on the bank for fulfilling this need. In Japan's underdeveloped labor market, where the most talented graduates are offered "lifetime" employment by the most prestigious firms and where the ability of new or mid-size firms to hire highly qualified graduates, particularly in financial and technical areas, is limited, the role of the bank in supplying personnel with financial expertise to those types of firms is crucial.

In the 1970s and earlier the acceptance of a *shukko* as a director may have been seen by some medium-size firms as a necessity to continue to secure the bank's loans to the firm at its best rates. Although in the 1990s this practice is no longer seen as necessary and the number of director *shukko* has greatly declined, the need for advisors with the skills of a *shukko* continues.[55]

In the past, a typical scenario would begin when a bank is asked by its client to send a senior banker for the number two position in its corporate finance department. The firm is anticipating the retirement of its own department head and provides informal assurances that the banker will eventually become a director within the company. The bank will then transfer an experienced and able senior employee who is not on the track for its own board of directors.[56] Thus, a vice president of the bank is likely to become at least a vice president of a major corporation or president or chair-

---

[55] Respondent #4 at Bank A: officer of a top six city bank.
[56] Respondent #2 formerly of Bank H: A former officer of a long-term credit bank.

man of one of its direct subsidiaries. In this manner the practice of *shukko* serves the bank by cementing a close bond between executives of the client firm and the bank who are now the firm's employees.

This one-way-ticket *shukko* functions primarily as an outplacement mechanism within Japan's lifetime employment system. Although people are usually retired in their mid-50s, the bank must find jobs for them after their retirement, at least until they are 60. A common pattern is for the bank to transfer out an employee in his 50s for a series of short-term assignments at different companies until he reaches the compulsory retirement age of 60, when he retires permanently to a position at a client company.[57]

Changes in the economy have upended the expectation that employees will be able to move up and out. Slower economic growth coupled with the creation of fewer new subsidiary companies, which in the past have served as locations to farm out employees, have led many corporations to become top heavy and to begin rationing the sharply reduced number of available directorial positions formerly reserved for their bank's retirees.[58] This problem for the banks has been particularly acute where bank mergers have occurred, which further limit the positions available in client companies and bank subsidiaries for an excessive number of redundant bank employees.[59]

Under the Japanese employment system, the wage scale is largely determined by length of service. Given the pyramid structure, employees in the upper levels have to leave so that the junior levels can move up. (See Figure 6.1: The career pyramid.)

This transfer mechanism enables the banks to move out higher-salaried senior employees not destined for top management positions within the bank to its mid-sized client firms in need of qualified senior financial executives, or to the bank's affiliated member companies in its *kigyo shudan* and its subsidiaries. Thus the *shukko* system is also effective in lowering the bank's payroll costs because banks are now using younger employees to perform relationship services formerly performed by higher-paid older employees.

---

[57] Respondent #1 at Bank D: An officer of a top six city bank.
[58] Respondent #1 at Bank C: An officer of a top six city bank.
[59] Respondent #1 at Bank C: An officer of a top six city bank.

Figure 6.1   The career pyramid

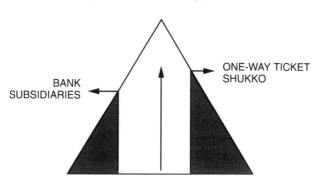

BANK
SUBSIDIARIES

ONE-WAY TICKET
SHUKKO

Respondent: If he's in his late 40s, then it's probably a move out. The bank is getting rid of relatively expensive people. The wage system is tied to seniority, and in banks where the average wage is ¥6 million, this person will be making ¥10 or 12 million by virtue of the fact that he has gotten older, so they try to farm him out.

Question: At a comparable salary?

Respondent: Not always. If they are farming him out to a subsidiary, his salary may go down 30%, but he doesn't have much choice in the matter. Then there is the opposite situation: someone in their late 40s who goes from Sanwa Bank to a very important position at Hitachi with an increase in salary. But, most of the time the banks are farming out, getting rid of expensive people. You also get your retirement pay up to that point, and it's taxed at a lower rate.[60]

The alternative for most large banks is to transfer senior employees to their facilities management company (back room operations) and bank-owned subsidiaries, such as leasing companies and other nonbank financial institutions.[61]

As Japanese firms continue to downsize in the 1990s there are fewer and fewer positions available in client firms for retirement

---

[60] Respondent #1: President of bank services organization.

Figure 6.2   The "bubble economy" career pyramid

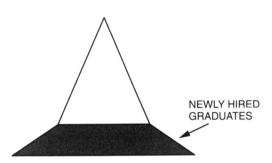

NEWLY HIRED
GRADUATES

shukko from the banks. Another result of the "bubble economy" of the 1980s was the hoarding mentality of the most prestigious firms, including banks, which led to the overhiring of new college graduates. (See Figure 6.2: The "bubble economy" career pyramid.) Now banks must outplace their mid-career employees at increasingly younger ages, either to client companies or to bank-owned subsidiaries with a cut in their pay.

The *Shukko* Employee's Conflict of Interest: Insider versus Outsider

Any inherent conflict of interest brought about by the *shukko* system is rarely acknowledged. Since *shukko* facilitates the flow of information back and forth between the client and the bank, sometimes inside information is revealed to the bank. Senior bankers stated that they saw no conflict since the information "was harmless if kept strictly between the bank and the client." Bankers said that *shukko* is seen as an expression of loyalty and commitment to a long-term relationship, which helps to build bonds of reliance and confidentiality between the company and the bank, and declared the main bank–client relationship non-competitive.[62]

---

[61] Respondent #1: President of bank services organization.

However, loyalty to the bank can appear to supersede acting in the client's best interest. For instance, a former bank employee now at the client firm may find it difficult not to accept a loan offer at a rate higher than the going rate because it is being made by his former bank. Companies, particularly small and medium-sized firms, are willing to trade off such conflicts of interest against the experience and skills they acquire by hiring bank retirees.[63] Although the bank may get an inside man in the retiree, the company, for its part, expects the assurance that the bank will provide the company with continued support no matter how bad it gets. One banker sardonically referred to the *shukko* employee as being "held hostage" by the client firm.[64]

On the other hand, those former bank employees who have been "seconded"—sent on a one-way-ticket *shukko,* must quickly transfer allegiance to their new firm or otherwise be isolated as a *soto*—an outsider, not an *uchi*—an insider. The covert resentment of fellow employees to the outside appointee is particularly common when the outsider is seen as coming in at the expense of an insider's advancement. Identity within the group and indeed within the context of the society at large is defined by issues of *soto* versus *uchi*. The strongest personal imperative of the seconded employee will be to cross the lines from *soto* to *uchi*, because it will determine his future within his new firm and whether he will be isolated from knowledge of sensitive matters and effective participation in the decision-making process. Any hint to his co-workers of divided loyalties between the firm and the former bank would be of the greatest detriment to his future career. For this reason alone, the longevity of his usefulness as an information conduit to the bank is quite limited, according to one former bank director, "a couple of years at most."[65]

Nevertheless, the *shukko* system tends to influence the bank–client relationship in such a way that it becomes virtually impossible to displace the main bank from its position. A rival banker from the client's second bank lamented that a practically insurmountable hurdle is created when the main bank "has sent over the years 50 to 60 people to a company, many of them executives in a position to

[62] Respondents #1 and #2 at Bank B: Officers of a top six city bank.
[63] Respondent #1 at Bank C: An officer of a top six city bank.
[64] Respondent #2 formerly of Bank H: A former officer of a long-term credit bank.

exclude other banks."[66] With such intimate personal ties at so many levels between the bank and its client, it becomes extremely problematic for a client firm even to contemplate a change of main bank. For this reason, Japanese banking is said to be a "skin-to-skin relationship."[67]

The main bank relationship is rooted in the history of the postwar reconstruction of the Japanese economy and, prior to that, in the role of the bank within the prewar *zaibatsu* groups. Indeed, much of its present-day practices stem from that history and also bear within them a strong component of traditional group relationships endogenous to Japanese society. Nonetheless, we cannot escape the fact that the functionalist practices of the main bank relationship are to seek competitive advantages in a system in which the relationship itself is a key source of bank profits.

---

[65] Respondent #1 at Bank G: A retired senior officer of a former specialized city bank.

[66] Respondent #1 at Bank I: An officer at a long-term credit bank.

[67] Respondent #1: Senior officer of a banking association.

7 Bank versus Firm: Triangulating the Data

BANK/FIRM: THE QUANTITATIVE DATA

In the previous chapter we reviewed the qualitative data, presenting our findings from interviews with bankers. Now we will also present quantitative evidence obtained from two large-scale surveys which, contemporaneously with our research, focused on many of the same or similar issues, but from the opposing perspective of the client firm. The Fuji Sogo Kenkyujo study [1993] surveyed corporate executives from 1,175 non-financial firms, including 329 firms from the First Section, 161 firms in the Second Section, 114 over-the-counter (OTC) traded firms, and 570 privately held firms. The Omura study surveyed 351 firms of the 1,501 listed on the First and Second Sections of the Tokyo Stock Exchange. We were also aided in our use of these studies by access to the researchers themselves in interpreting the findings. Comparison of the results drawn from our interview data with the hard numbers of the Fuji and Omura studies afforded the invaluable opportunity to triangulate two wholly different types of data, the qualitative data of the interviews with the quantitative data of the surveys, as well as the data from the banks with data from the firms, enabling us to achieve substantive triangulation for the principal findings of our study.

These results—from the comparison of both the qualitative and quantitative data—led to a fundamental redefinition of the main bank relationship, challenging basic assumptions as to its nature and the very reasons for its existence. Some commentators have predicted that the main bank system will ultimately disappear in Japan as a result of the liberalization process of financial markets, which presumably would undermine the close-knit ties inherent in those relationships. Proponents of that view cite the fact that bank lending to large corporations has decreased, now that the corporations have direct access to and are able to raise funds more cheaply in domestic and international money markets. However, as our most recent set of respondent interviews indicate, the banks themselves with the establishment of their own securities subsidiaries have assumed this role, displacing all but the top Big Four securities firms (Nomura, Daiwa, Nikko, and Yamaichi) as the leading underwriters of corporate bonds.

The respondents in our study reported that, rather than corporate lending, the main bank relationship *itself* is the bank's greatest source of profits. Indeed, the liberalization of interest rates in recent years has made large corporate lending the least profitable aspect of the banking business. Similarly, the competition between bank securities subsidiaries in underwriting corporate bonds has proven to be a low profit area and is considered by bankers as a "loss leader" necessary in maintaining client relationships. By contrast, as the respondents reported, a bank will ordinarily receive many lucrative benefits from its status as lead main bank to a company. The bank expects to be given the main deposit accounts of its client, and it will require, as well, that the client firm holds a standing low- or noninterest compensating balance account (formerly called *ryodate* account). The client may also be expected to maintain low-interest-bearing time deposits at the bank for some off–balance sheet favor such as a business introduction. In addition, the bank receives a disproportionately larger share of fee-based transactions such as transfers, foreign exchange, and derivative products, an important area of bank profits, than the other banks in the client firm's lending hierarchy. Finally, whether the client is large or small, the bank also expects to receive the advantage of the company's employee pool as its customers and with it the opportunity to supply a host of lucrative retail services to this captive client base. A single large company can lead to many hundreds, if not thousands, of personal accounts and employee customers for such bank services as personal loans, home mortgages, credit card, consumer lending, bill payments, and account transaction fees. These retail banking services are among the highest profit centers for banks today.

Our research suggests that the main bank system is no longer driven by large corporate bank borrowing. It has found new fuel in a host of bank products and services so that a main bank's relationship with its large clients remains quite profitable—for the main bank and for the second, third, fourth, and even fifth bank in the lending hierarchy as well.

These various forms of compensation by a client firm to its main bank are substantiated by the quantitative data reported by the Fuji Research survey of firm executives. Their results revealed that company executives had a keen awareness that much of the hidden costs of the main bank relationship are passed on to the firm's employees and to the firm itself through concessionaire accounts and by the reallocation of unreported costs to fee- and commission-based business. (See Figure 7.1: Firms report on how banks are compensated.)

As the graph shows, according to the Fuji Research survey, companies recognize that they are expected to provide increased business to their main bank. Overall, 23.3% of all firms reported that they maintained non-main deposit accounts (special accounts and time deposits) in order to compensate their main bank. The second most common method of compensation were employee accounts and payroll transfers which were cited by 16.7% of the firms. These two forms of compensation were considered most significant by First Section listed firms, which reported special deposit accounts and employee accounts at a higher rate—27.9% and 21.3% respectively—as compensation to their bank. This also confirmed our own findings based on banker interviews described in Chapter 6.

Other forms of compensation reported by all firms included higher effective interest rates resulting from compensating balance accounts (*ryodate*) accounts, 6.3%, and increased purchases and holding of the bank's stock, 6.1%. The response of First Section firms to these two questions were 8.8% and 7.5% respectively. Nearly 9% of the First Section firms reported paying trustee fees for the underwriting of their corporate bonds to their main bank as a form of compensation, a significant figure. This again confirmed our own findings in Chapter 6 that, for those firms which issue corporate bonds, main bank underwriting facilitation is replacing lending in determining main bank status.

Some 5.6% of the First Section firms reported hiring retired bank employees as a form of compensation to their main banks, as did

Figure 7.1   Firms report on how banks are compensated

Category	Data
1. Increased non-main operating account deposits	23.3% / 27.9% / 22.2% / 21.8% / 21.0%
2. Employee accounts and other transfers of payment	16.7% / 21.3% / 15.8% / 13.6% / 14.9%
3. Higher effective interest rate —"*ryodate* accounts"	6.3% / 8.8% / 4.4% / 1.8% / 6.4%
4. Increased shareholding by firm in bank's stock	6.1% / 7.5% / 5.1% / 5.5% / 5.6%
5. Unnecessary borrowing	3.6% / 2.8% / 4.4% / 2.7% / 4.1%
6. Trustee fees	3.5% / 8.8% / 1.9% / 0.9% / 1.4%
7. *Shukko* — hiring retired bank employees	2.9% / 5.6% / 3.8% / 0.9% / 1.4%
8. Other	0.5% / 0.3% / 1.3% / 0.0% / 0.4%

Legend:
- Aggregate response
- 1st Section listed firms
- 2nd Section listed firms
- Unlisted publicly-held firms
- Privately-held firms

Axis: 0% 5% 10% 15% 20% 25% 30%

Source: Translated by the author from the data of Fuji Sogo Kenkyujo [1993].

3.8% of the Second Section listed firms, both well above the nominal response from unlisted, i.e., OTC-traded, firms (0.9%), and privately-held firms (1.4%). Notably, "unnecessary borrowing" was reported by 4.4% of the Second Section listed firms and 4.1% of the privately-held firms, a rate 50% higher than those of the First Section listed firms (2.8%) and the unlisted firms (2.7%).

On the other side of the picture, interview respondents reported that firms, for their part, recognize the benefits gained from the mutual relationship and will also go to great lengths to maintain it. Firms expect to be able to rely on the bank's good offices to supply business information, consulting services, and, especially for the medium-size firms, the ever-important bank introductions to prospective clients or suppliers. Bankers reported that the client corporation will go to extraordinary lengths to protect the hierarchical standing of its lead main bank but that the practices associated with relationship banking are not restricted nor exclusive to the lead main bank and its client. The second and third lending banks of that company will attempt to provide similar services, as will even the fourth and fifth banks in the lending hierarchy, which may be composed of upwards of 20 to 30 banks if the corporation is large. Preservation of that hierarchy in a highly competitive environment is of paramount importance to the main bank, particularly since it receives a disproportionately large share of profits from the client than the other institutions in the hierarchy. In fact, when the top five lending banks typically supply only 50% of the firm's borrowed funds, they can still expect to receive almost 100% of the firm's fee-based transactions, such as foreign exchange, letters of credit and other trade or business-related credit guarantees, leasing and underwriting to their non-bank financial subsidiaries.

The Fuji Research data further support our contention that the old definition of the main bank as the firm's largest creditor has been supplanted by the new role of bond underwriter and the guarantor and/or trustee for firms issuing such corporate debt. (See Figure 7.2: Criteria used by client firms to define their main bank.) As the graph shows, 93.6% of all firms reported that the leading description used by firms which issue corporate debt to define their main bank is the bank which guarantees and underwrites the firm's bond issues. Some 90.3% reported that their main

Figure 7.2 Criteria used by client firms to define their main bank

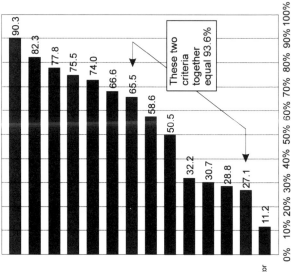

1. The bank which guarantees the firm's foreign bonds — 90.3
2. The bank which is largest lender among all other banks to the firm — 82.3
3. The bank which acknowledges its main bank status to the firm — 77.8
4. The bank's overseas securities subsidiary is co-manager underwriting the firm's foreign bonds — 75.5
5. The bank which gets the largest share of the firm's deposits — 74.0
6. The bank which has had the longest relationship with the firm — 66.6
7. The bank is a lead trustee for insuring bond issues of the firm among the trustee banks (but not a co-trustee) — 65.5
8. The bank with the largest share of the employees' salary accounts — 58.6
9. The largest shareholding bank of the company's stock — 50.5
10. The firm's president participates in the monthly Presidents Association meeting *shacho-kai* of the corporate group as the bank — 32.2
11. The bank which handles the largest share of foreign exchange transactions — 30.7
12. A former bank officer sits on the company's board of directors — 28.8
13. The bank is a trustee for the company's bond issue (excluding lead trustees counted in #7) — 27.1
14. There are former bank officers among the firm's employees, (not a director as in #12) — 11.2

These two criteria together equal 93.6%

0% 10% 20% 30% 40% 50% 60% 70% 80% 90% 100%

 Related to issuance of bonds. Companies which did not issue such corporate debt are not included in the calculation.

Source: Translated by the author from the data of Fuji Sogo Kenkyujo [1993].

bank was the bank which guarantees their foreign bonds.[68] As reported by 82.3% of the responding firms, this criterion has now eclipsed the definition of the main bank as the firm's largest lender among all its banks.

Again, there was a high correlation in the responses relating to how firms defined their main banks between the survey results and our findings from banker interviews detailed in Chapter 6. The survey criteria, paralleling those stated by the bankers, included: the bank with the largest share of the firm's deposits, 74.0%; the bank which has the longest relationship with the firm, 68.6%; and the bank with the largest share of employees' salary accounts, 58.6%.

By comparison, responses were significantly lower for some of the criteria which form the evidentiary base of agency theorists' conclusions, such as bank membership in the group's Presidents Association (*shacho-kai*—denoting *kigyo shudan* membership), 32.2%; a former bank employee sitting on the firm's board of directors, 28.8%; or former bank officers among the firm's employees, 11.2%.

As seen above, the survey findings provided repeated corroboration for the findings proposed by our independently developed qualitative data. The overall fit of the results of the two research approaches suggests some fundamental conclusions about the sum and substance of the main bank relationship.

The relationship between the main bank and its client firm must remain sufficiently flexible and responsive so as to meet the needs of both the bank and the firm. Both sides are aware that first and foremost each must satisfy the other's expectations. The nature of those expectations is defined by what each provides to the other. The firm provides its main deposit and compensating balance accounts as well as highly profitable access to its employees through their personal accounts and by extension their consumer banking needs. The bank provides a stable source of funding, which in the case of larger firms has come to mean their corporate bond underwriting facilities, and a whole host of business introductions and client advisory services. On the other hand, as we will now see, the firm considers the main bank an outsider when it comes to issues of

---

[68] The Fuji Sogo Kenkyujo survey was conducted during January 1993, before bank-owned securities subsidiaries were given permission to underwrite corporate bond issuance in the domestic market in 1994.

monitoring. Likewise, the bank will coldly examine its own position when the firm is facing solvency problems and is in need of life-saving financial support.

BANK GOVERNANCE: THE QUANTITATIVE DATA

The "Monitoring" Function of the Main Bank Relationship

Among the most scrutinized questions regarding the main bank system is the purported governance role of the main bank in relation to its client firm. Monitoring of the client firm by the bank team is often cited as evidence of the existence of such an external governance function. As the bankers reported, the bank works hard to maintain close bank-to-client relations. In the case of a large corporation, a bank team, typically headed by a relationship manager, is intimately involved in the affairs of the client, visiting the firm's offices and other facilities on a daily basis. This team is solely dedicated to that one assignment. Our respondents revealed, however, that the nature of the team's mission is essentially sales-oriented. The team's purpose is to try and obtain information about the firm's future plans in order to promote the bank's services. According to our respondents, a bank's ability to exercise any form of outside governance arises exclusively from its position as a major creditor and only when there are no other options for the client firm to access other banks, outside money markets, or internal sources of funds. However, given the competitive nature of the banking industry, other banks competing with the firm's main bank are usually only too eager to grant a new loan in an effort to improve their position in the lending hierarchy.

The main bank's leverage is therefore quite low over firms listed in the First Section of the Tokyo Stock Exchange (generally large capitalized firms) and even over Second Section firms (generally large to medium capitalized firms), because firms in both categories have direct access to money markets and thus can circumvent the need for bank finance. Indeed, it is difficult for banks to monitor the activities of many such firms due to these firms' large scope of operations, business locations, and the multitude of other banks a firm may deal with.

When firms are of mid- to small-size and are unlisted (OTC-publicly traded firms and privately held firms), banks are most often unable to provide the scrutiny required to monitor because of the insufficient numbers of bank personnel assigned to service this category of firm. The often closed nature of privately held firms, which are usually controlled by the firm's founder and family, also precludes bank monitoring. As reported by our respondents, in such smaller-sized firms, unless the president-owner comes to the bank for additional credit assistance under distressed circumstances, the bank is often unaware of any current undisclosed problems. At this point, the bank must make the judgment of whether a workout is worthwhile or even possible from the business perspective of the bank. Unlike the case of a large firm in which the bank may have a greater stake as a creditor, for small-sized and privately held firms the possibility of rescue by the main bank does not exist and the best the firm can hope for is some bank-arranged takeover by another firm. Aware of such consequences, the head of such a distressed closely-held firm typically loathes the bank's interference and often tries to cover up or forestall the reporting of difficulties. Only if the bank has been monitoring for abnormalities in the cash flows of a firm's deposit accounts might it be able to catch any hint of trouble, but by this time any corrective action or even the bank's withdrawal of lending could be too late. In those cases it simply becomes a race by the bank to seize the firm's collateral before other creditors get wind of the impending failure.

The Purported "Signaling" Function of the Main Bank

According to agency theorists, other creditors take their cues by observing the "signals" of the main bank's actions, stemming from its position as the firm's largest creditor [Hoshi *et al.*, 1990a, 1990b; Sheard, 1989, 1991; Aoki 1990]. This of course begs the question, as our interview data revealed, of whether the signal "sent" was necessarily an accurate representation of the client firm's actual internal affairs. Often the signal is distorted by the main bank's own strategic considerations and needs in maintaining a particular client relationship. Sick patients can be very profitable (higher interest rates, increased guarantee fees, etc.); dead patients not at all.

However, any hint of trouble, signaled by a decrease in lending by the firm's main bank, would indeed be noted by the other creditors, typically setting off a chain reaction of retreat by those banks which benefit least from their relationship with the ailing firm.

Bankers reported that the main bank was often the lender of "last resort" to a firm only because the other creditors had been able to accomplish a rapid retreat, thereby increasing the burden of the main bank(s). Main banks were therefore very keen on *not* sending any signal which would lead to the collapse of the firm's lending syndicate. That is why competing banks prudently make their own independent credit assessments—*caveat creditor.*

Main Bank Governance Through Cross-Shareholding?

Cross-shareholding between the bank and the client firm is another often-cited evidence of the main bank's governance function. Agency theorists have paid most attention to the cross-shareholding relationship between firms and financial institutions, specifically ascribing the central role in governance to the main bank [Sheard, 1991, 1994b]. Other shareholders are then able to "free ride" on the main bank's alleged monitoring activities. However, the questionnaire data [Fuji Sogo Kenkyujo, 1993; Omura, 1993] further support the reports of our banker respondents that any presumed free-riding action by other cross-shareholders is irrelevant. The results of the two questionnaire surveys, which studied the firms' perspectives on their main banks as reported by corporate executives, clearly demonstrate that non-financial company managers do not regard mutual stock ownership in investment terms but more often as mutual security and non-aggression pacts. The nature of cross-shareholding is such that in most situations the other cross-share-holders are neither free to sell their shares nor free to exercise ownership rights over recalcitrant managers (agents) of the other firm because cross-shareholding arrangements in general have *anti*-governance, rather than governance, expectations built into them. Indeed, they themselves (as agents) in their own firms have made a non-interference pact with those very same managers of the other firms to protect their own incumbency.

It is thus not surprising that the firms in both the Fuji Sogo

Kenkyujo and Omura surveys reported they maintained a distinct preference for *not* selecting a bank when choosing stable shareholders. Privately held firms viewed their fellow non-financial "group" members as their most reliable shareholders. The stable shareholders most preferred by listed firms (and second most preferred by privately held firms) were companies which were outside the banks and other financial institutions or even their own group members, thus enabling them to avoid the web of transaction expectations and obligations that often come with these types of institutional partners. Some 406 out of 507 (80%) privately held firms in the Fuji Sogo Kenkyujo [1993] survey reported that they had no stable shareholding relations with banks, compared with only 101 (16%) of the 604 publicly traded respondents. On the other hand, for the non-financial firms which did have cross-shareholding relations with banks, 64% of these firms expressed concern about the falling share prices of the bank stocks they held (as did 78% of those firms which were having their own share price difficulties) [Omura, 1993], and holding these bank shares was seen by firms as a burden rather than a benefit. Much of those bank shares were bought during the late 1980s when client firms were importuned by their banks to purchase their shares as banks sought to raise capital to meet BIS requirements as to their capital adequacy ratio.

The Omura data [1993] further revealed that the only firms which valued their cross-shareholding relationships with financial institutions more than with non-financial shareholding partners were those firms that were highly dependent upon banks. This category of firm was indicated by such negative factors as: relatively small size of capital; low efficiency of capital ratio (pretax income/total capital); low capital/assets ratio; low capital growth; large losses in the firm's stock price; and low concentrations of ownership. Another key bank dependency factor reported by Omura was the general negative health of the particular industry to which the firm belonged, for example, publicly traded companies in such ailing industries as iron and steel and, to a lesser degree, machine tools, electrical machinery, trading firms, and the services industries. The healthy (at the time of the survey) high cross-shareholding automotive industry respondent companies saw cross-shareholding relations with financial institutions as much less beneficial than those with their own *keiretsu* or "group" affiliated companies.

Attitudes toward share ownership had been undergoing a re-assessment in the early 1990s. However, after a brief period of rising expectations for change, issues of corporate governance have for the present all but died. Nevertheless, a majority of publicly held firms are expecting that the demand for increased dividends by their stable shareholders will grow, whereas in the past, especially among the First Section and the OTC firms, a policy of increased capital gains in lieu of dividends had sufficed. Some 79.3% of First Section firms said that they expected to be increasing their dividends. There is a growing realization, however, that there are too few options for the implementation of fundamental changes in dividend policy during the presently depressed economy. Indeed, the majority of responses from privately held firms indicated the expectation that the demand for dividends by their stable shareholders will not increase, and that they will continue to rely solely on capital gains for their compensation policy [Fuji Sogo Kenkyujo, 1993]. With shareholders demanding more accountability from corporate managers, the majority of publicly traded firms conceded that it was "somewhat necessary" to disclose information to individual investors but saw their annual financial statement as sufficiently informative. Of the privately held firms 71.6% saw no necessity for disclosure whatsoever. Beyond what was reported in their annual statement few companies saw any need to explain their policies for distribution of profits, management of capital expenditures, or future project plans [Fuji Sogo Kenkyujo, 1993].

The *Uchi–Soto* Continuum and Main Bank Governance

If we examine the responses of corporate executives to the Fuji Sogo Kenkyujo survey as to who should be provided access to the firms' financial reports, a key element for effective corporate governance, we can see that firms view the bank as relatively distant in terms of insider versus outsider graded relationships. Banks are clearly seen in the eyes of management more as outsiders than as insiders. (See Figure 7.3: Firms report on who is entitled to monitor.) The graph of the Fuji Research survey of firms shows a progression among a host of possible stakeholders, from those who management feels are entitled to monitor to those it feels are not so entitled. This progression from internal auditor, highest ranked as entitled to monitor, on down is analogous to the *uchi–soto* continuum, each category reflecting its respective position as an insider or an outsider in relationship to the firm. Among those stakeholders, some 21.6% of the company executives surveyed felt that the main bank was not entitled to monitor compared with only 11.1% who thought the main bank was entitled. Indeed, this rejection of the main bank's purported agency role was even more evident among the responding firms listed in the First Section of the Tokyo Stock Exchange; there only 4.3% of executives felt that the main bank was entitled to monitor whereas some 24.8% felt the main bank was not so entitled, clearly casting the bank in the role of *soto*—an outsider to the firm.

DATA AND THEORY BUILDING: AN ITERATIVE PROCESS

The development of theory can be said to be a highly iterative process. Does the data, both qualitative and quantitative, support the theory? Does the theory support the data? Continual testing and retesting are required. Out of our experience with this process came the need to reconcile the pecuniary goals of the bank, which the interview data stressed, with the historical evidence relating to the origins of the Japanese firm and the bank's purported role in the *kigyo shudan*. Certain assumptions fundamental to the Nakatani–Hoshi–Aoki–Sheard thesis were thus challenged. These included, first, the bank's central role as a group member and, second, the bank's purported governance role within the group. The qualitative and quantitative data we examined cast serious doubts about these two propositions, which completely ignored the intense competitiveness that exists among Japanese banks and the extent to which a bank's role is confined by its limited relational access.

To reconcile this apparent divergence with what had become the commonly accepted theory, it became necessary to develop a better understanding of the bank's relationship to its client firms, and to place it within a broader context than the reductionist approaches that agency theory or transaction cost analysis would allow or could explain. Communal organizational theories of the fief and the clan were more appropriate to a description of a Japanese model because they included considerations of cultural context. The inclusion of

Figure 7.3   Firms report on who is entitled to monitor

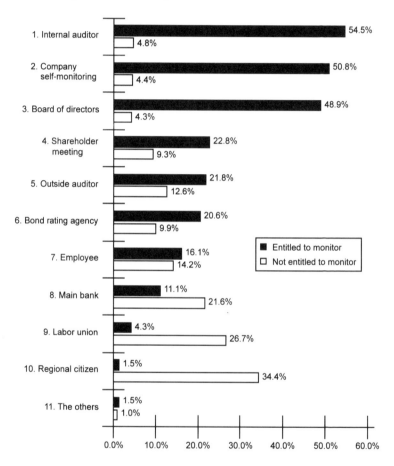

Source: Translated by the author from the data of Fuji Sogo Kenkyujo [1993].

context changed the linear market/hierarchy dichotomy into a more complex four-quadrant matrix. This matrix was in essence a Cartesian plane based upon information diffusion as the *x*-axis, and information codification as the *y*-axis. (See Figure 3.1 in Chapter 3.) These theories, however, still did not fully account for the hypothesis that the bank maintained a status of centrality that went far beyond the transaction requirements of a credit-based system of finance. Nor were communal theories able to account for the qualitative and quantitative data of our research findings which revealed that the bank was not as central as the Nakatani–Hoshi–Aoki–Sheard thesis had led so many to believe. In our findings we determined that: (1) the main bank relationship was viewed by client firms to be more of an advantage to the bank; (2) only firms which were relatively more dependent upon bank financing considered cross-shareholding with financial institutions more important than with group member non-financial firms; (3) the bank exploited the relative dependency of such firms to its own advantage; (4) traditional patterns of firm relationships often masked the asymmetrical character of these relationships from the scrutiny of outsiders (and researchers); and (5) only from the careful analysis of these sets and subsets of interfirm relationships could it be determined whether the relationship was relatively synergistic or relatively exploitative.

The development of the relational access dimension within communal theories of the firm and its group required going beyond merely tabulating the exploitation of traditional patterns of relationships. Through the iterative process of repeatedly juxtaposing our conflicting evidence with the accepted theory, we were able to develop the general principles for a concept of relational access which transforms the communal view of interfirm relationships beyond a four-quadrant Cartesian plane. This concept defines a new intersecting plane, which we characterize as a third dimension, in our theory—The Relational Access Paradigm. (See Figure 3.3 Chapter 3.) This dimension describes a paramount priority of our intra- and interfirm Japanese model, the necessity to define all relationships along an *uchi–soto* (insider–outsider) continuum.

8 Conclusion

In our analysis of the Japanese firm and industrial group relations we have argued that core Japanese business practices are determined by sets of uncodified rules and obligations that are opaque to outsider scrutiny. The governing principle underlying these practices is described as "relational access," a continuum of relationship from insider to outsider by which inter- and intrafirm relations are determined.

Based upon this concept, we have presented a new model of Japanese firm and industrial group relations which we have termed the "Relational Access Paradigm." The paradigm proposes an *r*-dimension, an *uchi–soto* (insider–outsider) continuum which defines where one firms stands in relation to another. The paradigm intentionally extends the concept of the firm and group firms beyond the boundaries drawn by *de jure* property rights theories to encompass a concept of the firm and group as participants in an arena of collective action in which viability as an institution is greatly dependent on the supportive milieu in which the firm and its group are situated. In this sense, we view the Japanese firm and group as a nexus of *implicit relational* contracts, indicative of a high-context, communal form of industrial organization, in contradistinction to the firm as a nexus of linear contracts in a freely negotiated market.

Central to our model of the Japanese firm is a graded pattern of concentric relationships traceable from the *ie*-style merchant household of Tokugawa Japan to today's corporate relationships and the *kigyo shudan* and *keiretsu* industrial group forms. Within the concentric spheres, issues of ranking, relatedness, and identification as either *uchi* (insider) or *soto* (outsider) are as significant today as they were four hundred or more years ago. In our view the formation of the production unit in Japan remains fundamentally coextensive with an elaborated meaning of kinship and household, and with the loyalties and allegiances which those inspire.

131

In describing the historical antecedents that prepared the way for the great trading houses and their commercial banks, known as the *zaibatsu* in the prewar period, we have sought to demonstrate how their earlier "house" practices not only prefigured relationships within the six large corporate enterprise groups (*kigyo shudan*) of today, but, more significantly, are also prototypic of the formation of relationships within industrial groups, both big and small, throughout Japanese society and its economy. Although some scholars trace the origins of these practices only as far back as the prewar *zaibatsu*, we believe they can be shown to relate back to early seventeenth-century Japanese social values and to the cultural mores that prevailed for a millennium and more before. Similarly, our discussion of the *ie* (household) attempted not only to set forth some of the historical antecedents of modern Japanese managerial practices but, more fundamentally, to propose that a deeper, more culturally inclusive view of the nature of relationships among Japanese firms and their industrial groups is critical to the current analysis of the Japanese firm.

We have argued that the agency approach to the Japanese industrial groups and particularly the main bank relationship has been based upon a number of false assumptions, most frequently relating to three areas: corporate governance by the *shacho-kai* or Presidents Associations; main bank monitoring, chiefly by the bank team sent to the client firm; and the practice known as *shukko*, which includes the appointment of outside directors to a firm's board by its main bank.

As we see it, the failure of the proponents of agency theory to discern the nature of the *shacho-kai* arises from not drawing clear distinctions between the collegial relationships within the *kigyo shudan*, i.e., the clan form, and the hierarchical relationships of the *keiretsu*, i.e., the fief form. Misplaced assumptions relating to main bank monitoring by the bank team likewise stem from the failure to understand the nature and abilities of the bank team, particularly as to its overriding sales function, that is, to promote new business. During the "bubble period" of the 1980s the mission of the bank teams was primarily to boost bank assets by issuing new loans, which were often used for speculative purposes by the client. This lending/sales function was in obvious conflict with agency theory notions of monitoring a client firm's creditworthiness, which the bank could do only to a very limited extent in any case. Furthermore, today, as in the past, only the largest corporations merit their own bank teams. Medium and small-sized firms receive only the occasional attentions of already overburdened junior officers whose ability to monitor their client firms is often limited to tracking the cash flow into the client's main deposit account.

The agency assumption of firm monitoring by former bankers, the so-called *shukko* process, is similarly flawed. As discussed, *shukko* reflects the primarily fiscal necessity of the bank to find early retirement positions for high-salaried senior bank executives and only secondarily may operate to influence a client firm's management. In our study, bankers readily acknowledged that their continued influence over their former employees was extremely limited, if not nil, when a conflict of interest arose between the bank and its client firm. The necessity to retire senior bank employees has accelerated in pace since the overhiring of junior personnel during the "bubble period."

In considering the role of banks in corporate governance, we conclude that banks are not acting as monitors in the agency sense, that is, as agents for fellow shareholders, since the bank's own credit exposure to the client far exceeds its own equity position in the client firm. Even from a creditor's standpoint, the bank's ability to monitor is limited. The current banking crisis in Japan has painfully revealed the banks' less than minimal ability to evaluate the creditworthiness of clients when money was lent to pursue land and stock speculations in the 1980s.

Another key agency assumption of bank governance are the so-called bank rescues. Our evidence reveals that they generally have been effected only when the bank determined that a client's difficulties were a result of a liquidity problem rather than a solvency crisis—and then it acted out of its own interest, if not just for its own profit. However, as a number of bank officers reported, they were often the last to know of an imminent financial crisis when the client firm was intent on evading bank oversight. If the main bank rescue function really did exist, such calculated evasion by failing client firms would have been pointless at the very least, if not counterproductive. In cases of insolvency, "rescue" most often means overseeing the dissolution of the firm's assets and the distribution of collateral to its chief creditors, namely, the banks. Only in those limited cases deemed by governmental authorities to be in the interest of the nation's welfare does the Ministry of Finance "request" a main bank to deliver a rescue package.

In the ever-rising economy which had been characteristic of Japan in the postwar era, the validity of agency assumptions of internal corporate governance, issues of "self-governance," and the main bank's "rescue function," implicit or otherwise, had not been seriously tested. Now, as Japan suffers its first profound postwar recession, questions of corporate efficiency are being starkly confronted. In a sense this recession can be and with increasing frequency is characterized as a "governance recession." For shareholders, return on investment is no longer being satisfied by capital gains. Furthermore, banks and other financial institutions are no longer able to rely on the size and growth of assets as a reliable indicator of the soundness of their institutions. Rather, for banks ROA and quality of assets have become the watchwords of the "post-bubble economy."

The persistence of the current economic recession in Japan has led some observers to speculate that there will be a winding down of the cross-shareholding system as hard-pressed companies are forced to take capital gains from the sale of cross-held shares in order to dress up their bottom lines. However, among companies holding such shares, the required fiscal reports for the year ending March 31, 1993 revealed a slight *increase* in cross-shareholding patterns [Mabuchi, 1993; Kumagai, 1994]. Indeed, it has been a very common practice for banks and other cross-shareholders, in an attempt to capture profits to dress up their annual statements, to sell and then immediately repurchase these shares at the current market price to realize the capital gains, thus leaving intact their ratio of cross-held shares. That many of these cross-held shares were originally acquired as an exchange, and represent nothing more than paper transactions without any injection of new capital to either firm, raises the specter that the cross-shareholding system, aside from management's anti-governance objectives, may be a house of cards ready to collapse with serious consequences for the equity market, should any large-scale sell-off of cross-held shares be attempted. This leads us to conclude that the cross-shareholding system's objectives are other than for investment purposes.

That banks feel obliged to repurchase these shares is indicative of the fact that the purpose of this shareholding is strictly relational access, a necessary component for their maintaining close transactional ties to client firms, similar to the close vendor/supplier relations that non-financial companies also must maintain with their cross-shareholding business partners. As one banker reported to the author, his bank's sale of any client shares requires the assessment of the relationship and approval of three departments before they may be sold.

In today's market far fewer gains can be captured by selling off shares. Indeed, it depends when those shares were initially acquired. For many banks, their so-called "hidden assets" are in fact unrealized losses, since those share were initially purchased during the boom markets of the 1980s, or last repurchased for capital gains at a higher levels. If shares are sold for fundraising, then some care should also be taken to distinguish between the cross-held relational shares and those shares which were purchased by corporations as speculative investments during the *zaitech* era—the period of financial "engineering" of the late 1980s. Although the rationalization of speculative investments from the *zaitech* era is to be expected, shares which were acquired as part of a cross-shareholding pattern based upon customer-supplier relationships are of a quite different character and purpose.

In sum, many of the supposed rationales of the mutual stockholding relationship, such as reduced share price volatility, are now in serious dispute. Other so-called benefits, such as the "smoothness" of shareholder meetings (the result of management steamrolling tactics), act primarily to protect management incumbency and are often explicitly anti-governance. Responses by corporate executives to the questions of the Fuji Sogo Kenkyujo [1993] and Omura [1993] surveys indicate that corporate governance concerns have had little or no impact on cross-shareholding patterns and show no evidence of a devolution of mutual shareholding arrangements. Thus, we can conclude only one significant purpose remains for maintaining stable business relationships, i.e., transactional relations between the cross-shareholding partner companies—as a franchise to do business with each other. This conclusion is in itself significant since these cross-held shares provide us here with what otherwise seldom exists, tangible evidence of implicit relational contracts.

The concept of the ownership of the firm is poorly developed in the literatures of economics and management. In the case of Japan, economics-based theories which view the firm as essentially a commodity, i.e., a bundle of rights with marketable value linked to an expected profit stream, inevitably collide with management-based theories in which forces of collectivity overwhelm pecuniary factors. Whereas in the West the joint-stock company weakened the role of the household firm, recasting it in essentially commodity terms, through the *ie*-system the Japanese firm was able to accomplish some of the same objectives as the joint-stock company while retaining the motivational aspects of a family business.

That Japanese business relationships still fall within this traditional pattern should not be perceived as an historical accident but rather as evidence that such a social system continues to be a necessary element in the success of Japanese capitalism. In the hierarchical *keiretsu* form, the web of traditional relations can become a vast reservoir within which asymmetries of power are able to exploit ingrained societal relations. In the hypothesis of perfect markets these asymmetries are vitiated, and such traditional reserves of relational obligations do not exist to be tapped in low-context, contractual societies. In a pure-market hypothesis in which everyone is a free agent and all of life is reduced to a series of spot transactions, all asymmetries and the opportunity for exploitation of these asymmetries theoretically is quickly lost to some free market equilibrium.

What has made Japanese capitalism so successful is that it has been able to tap into a traditional culture that supports the great exploitation of asymmetries, such as imperfect labor markets, to concentrate wealth. Although the opaque nature of *keiretsu* transactions has led some to presume that they are not dictated by power relationships between the parties and that such relations have no effect on price or exploitation, we conclude this view underestimates the fact that the essence of Japanese governance structures is not always predominantly synergistic, as the *kigyo shudan* form tends to be, but, as evidenced by the *keiretsu* form, is often rooted in the exploitation of asymmetries of information, labor, and a host of other variables in the sets and subsets of relationships that permeate

Japanese society. Our holistic model, the Relational Access Paradigm, provides a framework to better understand the dimensions of power, information, and access that define Japanese governance structures.

Appendix: Uni-Dimensional Schema of Industrial Group

This schema of Mitsui *zaibatsu* companies drawn by General Head-quarters of the Supreme Commander of Allied Powers, February 1946, is shown in Figure A.1 overleaf. This type of diagram is prototypic of those used to represent Japanese industrial groups.

Figure A.1   Typical uni-dimensional schema used to represent industrial groupings

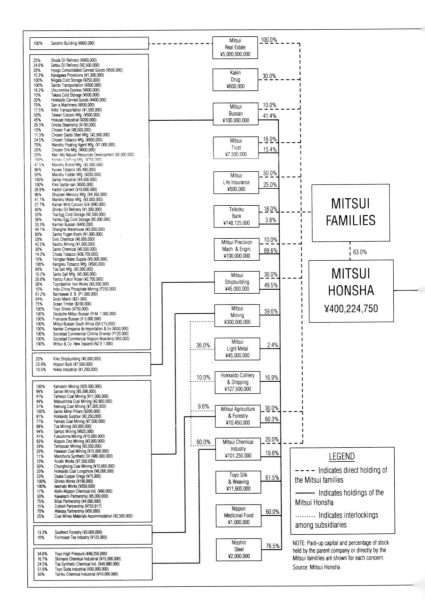

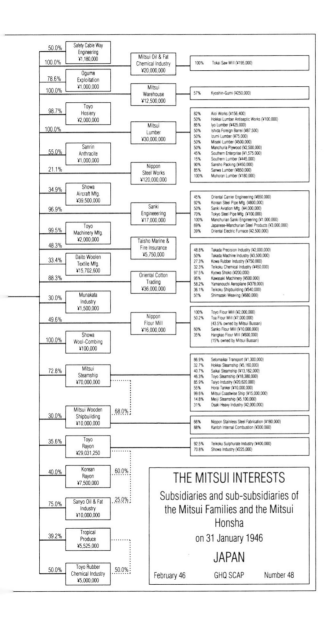

50.0%	Safety Cable Way Engineering ¥1,180,000	
100.0%		Mitsui Oil & Fat Chemical Industry ¥20,000,000
78.6%	Oguma Exploitation ¥1,000,000	
100.0%		Mitsui Warehouse ¥12,500,000
98.7%	Toyo Hosiery ¥2,000,000	
100.0%		Mitsui Lumber ¥30,000,000
55.0%	Sanrin Anthracite ¥1,000,000	
21.1%		Nippon Steel Works ¥120,000,000
34.9%	Showa Aircraft Mfg. ¥39,500,000	
96.9%		Sanki Engineeering ¥17,000,000
99.5%	Toyo Machinery Mfg. ¥2,000,000	
48.3%		Taisho Marine & Fire Insurance ¥5,750,000
33.4%	Daito Woolen Textile Mfg. ¥15,702,600	
88.3%		Oriental Cotton Trading ¥36,000,000
30.0%	Munakata Industry ¥1,500,000	
49.6%		Nippon Flour Mill ¥16,000,000
100.0%	Showa Wool-Combing ¥100,000	
72.8%	Mitsui Steamship ¥70,000,000	
30.0%	Mitsui Wooden Shipbuilding ¥10,000,000	68.0%
35.6%	Toyo Rayon ¥29,031,250	
40.0%	Korean Rayon ¥7,500,000	60.0%
75.0%	Sanyo Oil & Fat Industry ¥10,000,000	25.0%
39.2%	Tropical Produce ¥5,525,000	
50.0%	Toyo Rubber Chemical Industry ¥5,000,000	50.0%

100% Tokai Saw Mill (¥195,000)

57% Kyoshin-Gumi (¥250,000)

82% Aioi Works (¥156,400)
50% Hokkai Lumber Antiseptic Works (¥100,000)
85% Iyo Lumber (¥425,000)
50% Ishida Foreign Barrel (¥87,500)
50% Izumi Lumber (¥75,000)
50% Miseki Lumber (¥500,000)
50% Manchuria Plywood (¥2,500,000)
45% Southern Enterprise (¥1,575,000)
15% Southern Lumber (¥445,000)
90% Sansho Packing (¥450,000)
85% Sanwa Lumber (¥850,000)
100% Muhoran Lumber (¥180,000)

45% Oriental Carrier Engineering (¥650,000)
92% Korean Steel Pipe Mfg. (¥800,000)
50% Sanki Aviation Mfg. (¥4,000,000)
70% Tokyo Steel Pipe Mfg. (¥100,000)
100% Manchurian Sanki Engineering (¥1,000,000)
69% Japanese-Manchurian Steel Products (¥3,000,000)
39% Oriental Electric Furnace (¥2,500,000)

48.8% Takada Precision Industry (¥2,000,000)
50% Takada Machine Industry (¥3,500,000)
27.3% Kowa Rubber Industry (¥750,000)
32.3% Teikoku Chemical Industry (¥450,000)
97.5% Kyowa Shoko (¥200,000)
95% Kawasaki Machinery (¥500,000)
58.2% Yamanouchi Aeroplane (¥378,000)
36.1% Teikoku Shipbuilding (¥540,000)
50% Shimazaki Weaving (¥680,000)

100% Toyo Flour Mill (¥2,000,000)
50.2% Toa Flour Mill (¥7,000,000)
(43.5% owned by Mitsui Bussan)
60% Sanko Flour Mill (¥10,000,000)
35% Hangkao Flour Mill (¥600,000)
(15% owned by Mitsui Bussan)

86.9% Setomaikai Transport (¥1,300,000)
32.7% Hokkai Steamship (¥5,160,000)
40.7% Saikai Steamship (¥13,162,000)
46.3% Toyo Steamship (¥18,380,000)
85.9% Taiyo Industry (¥20,620,000)
55% Horai Tanker (¥10,000,000)
99.6% Mitsui Coastwise Ship (¥15,000,000)
14.8% Meiji Steamship (¥5,100,000)
31% Osaki Heavy Industry (¥2,000,000)

66% Nippon Stainless Steel Fabrication (¥180,000)
88% Kantoh Internal Combustion (¥300,000)

92.5% Teikoku Sulphurate Industry (¥400,000)
70.8% Showa Industry (¥225,000)

THE MITSUI INTERESTS

Subsidiaries and sub-subsidiaries of
the Mitsui Families and the Mitsui
Honsha
on 31 January 1946

JAPAN

February 46   GHQ SCAP   Number 48

References

Alchian, Armen A. and Harold Demsetz [1972] "Production, Information Costs, and Economic Organization," *American Economic Review*, 62: 777–95.

Aoki Masahiko [1984a] *The Co-operative Game Theory of the Firm*. Oxford: Oxford University Press.

— [1984b] "Aspects of the Japanese Firm," in M. Aoki (ed.) *The Economic Analysis of the Japanese Firm*, 3–43. North-Holland: Elsevier.

— [1987] "The Japanese Firm in Transition," in K. Yamamura and Y. Yasuba (eds) *The Political Economy of Japan*, 263–88. Stanford, CA: Stanford University Press.

— [1990] "Toward an Economic Model of the Japanese Firm," *Journal of Economic Literature*, 28 (March): 1–27.

— [1994] "Monitoring Characteristics of the Main Bank System: An Analytical and Developmental View," in M. Aoki and H. Patrick (eds) *The Japanese Main Bank System: Its Relevancy for Developing and Transforming Economies*. Oxford: Oxford University Press.

Aoki Masahiko and Hugh Patrick (eds) [1994] *The Japanese Main Bank System: Its Relevancy for Developing and Transforming Economies*. Oxford: Oxford University Press.

Asajima Shoichi [1984] "Financing of the Japanese Zaibatsu: Sumitomo as a Case Study," in A. Okochi and S. Yasuoka (eds) *Family Business in the Era of Industrial Growth, Its Ownership and Management*. Tokyo: University of Tokyo Press.

Bailey, Kenneth D. [1978] *Methods of Social Research*. New York: Free Press.

Barney, Jay B. and William G. Ouchi [1984] "Information Cost and Organization of Transaction Governance," unpublished manuscript, Graduate School of Management, University of California Los Angeles.

Baums, Theodor [1994] "The German Banking System and Its Impact on Corporate Governance and Finance," in M. Aoki and H. Patrick (eds) *The Japanese Main Bank System: Its Relevancy for Developing and Transforming Economies*. Oxford: Oxford University Press.

Bellah, Robert N. [1957] *Tokugawa Religion: The Values of Pre-Industrial Japan*. Boston: Beacon Press.

Bennett, John W. and Ishino Iwao [1963] *Paternalism in the Japanese Economy: Anthropological Studies of Oyabun-Kobun Patterns*. Minneapolis: University of Minnesota Press.

Berle, Adolph A. and G.C. Means [1932] *The Modern Corporation and Private Property*. New York: Macmillan.

Boisot, Max H. [1986] "Markets and Hierarchies in a Cultural Perspective," *Organization Studies*, 7: 135–8.

Boisot, Max H. and John Child [1988] "The Iron Law of Fiefs: Bureaucratic Failure and the Problem of Governance in the Chinese Economic Reforms," *Administrative Science Quarterly*, 33: 507–27

Burt, David N. and Michael F. Doyle [1993] *The American Keiretsu: Strategic Weapon for Global Competitiveness*. Homewood, IL: Irwin Publishing.

Business Week [1992] "American Keiretsu, Learning From Japan," cover story, January 27: 52–60.

Cable, J.R. [1985] "Capital Market Information and Industrial Performance: The Role of West German Banks," *Economic Journal*, 95: 118–32.

Carrington, J.C. and G.T. Edwards [1979] *Financing Industrial Investment*. London: Macmillan.

Coase, Ronald [1937] "The Nature of the Firm," *Econometrica* 4: 386–405.

Crafts, N.F.R. [1992] "Productivity Growth Reconsidered," *Economic Policy*, 15: 387–414.

Demsetz, Harold [1967] "Toward a Theory of Property Rights," *American Economic Association*, May: 347–59.

Diamond, Douglas W. [1984] "Financial Intermediation amd Delegated Monitoring," *Review of Economic Studies*, 51: 393–414.

Dore, Ronald [1987] *Taking Japan Seriously*. Stanford, CA: Stanford University Press.

Durkheim, Emile [1893/1933] (*De la division du travail social*) *The Division of Labor in Society*, G. Simpson trans. New York: Free Press.

Edwards, Jeremy E. and Klaus Fischer [1994] *Banks, Finance and Investment in Germany*. Cambridge: Cambridge University Press.

Eisenhardt, Kathleen M. [1989] "Building Theories from Case Study Research," *Academy of Management Review*, 14: 532–50.

Ferguson, Charles [1990] "Computers and the Coming of the U.S. Keiretsu," *Harvard Business Review*, July-August: 55–70.

Fruin, W. Mark [1992] *The Japanese Enterprise System*. New York: Oxford University Press.

Fuji Sogo Kenkyujo [1993] *Main bank system oyobi kabushiki ni tsuite no chosa* (An investigation regarding the influence of shareholding on the main bank system), research report. Tokyo.

Gerlach, Michael [1992] *Alliance Capitalism: The Social Organization of Japanese Business*. Berkeley: University of California Press.

Gilson, Ronald and M. Roe [1993] "Understanding the Japanese Keiretsu: Overlaps Between Corporate Governance and Industrial Organization," *Yale Law Journal*, 102: 871–906.

Glaser, Barney G. and Anselm L. Strauss [1967] *The Discovery of Grounded Theory: Strategies for Qualitative Research*. Chicago: Aldine Publishing.

Gouldner, Alvin W [1960] "The Norm of Reciprocity," *American Sociological Review*, 25: 161–78.

Granovetter, Mark [1985] "Economic Action and Social Structure: The Problem of Embeddedness," *American Journal of Sociology*, 91: 481–510.

Hadley, Eleanor M. [1970] *Anti-Trust in Japan*, Princeton, NJ: Princeton University Press.

Hall, Edward T. [1977] *Beyond Culture*. Garden City, NY: Doubleday.

Hall, Edward T. and Mildred Hall [1990] *Understanding Cultural Differences*. Yarmouth, ME: Intercultural Press.

Hart, Oliver [1989] "An Economist's Perspective on the Theory of the Firm," *Columbia Law Review*, 89 (November): 1757–74.

Harvard Business Review [1990] "Can a Keiretsu Work in America?: An Exchange of Letters," September–October: 180–96.

Hattori Tamio [1984] "The Relationship between Zaibatsu and Family Structure: The Korean Case," in A. Okochi and S. Yasuoka (eds) *Family Business in the Era of Industrial Growth, Its Ownership and Management*. Tokyo: University of Tokyo Press.

Hofstede, Geert H. [1991] *Cultures and Organizations: Software of the Mind*. Maidenhead: McGraw-Hill (UK).

Horie Yasuzo [1966] "The Role of the *Ie* in the Economic Modernization of Japan," *Kyoto University Economic Review*, 36 (1): 1–16.

— [1977] "The Tradition of *Ie* (House) and the Industrialization of Japan," in K. Nakagawa (ed.) *Social Order and Entrepreneurship*, 231–54. Tokyo: University of Tokyo Press.

Horiuchi Akiyoshi [1989] "Informational Properties of the Japanese Financial System," *Japan and the World Economy*, 1 (3): 255–78.

— [1993] "Financial Structure and Managerial Discretion in the Japanese Firm: An Implication of the Surge of Equity-Related Bonds," unpublished paper, revised October 1993.

— [1995] "Financial Sector Reforms in Postwar Japan," unpublished paper, October.

Horiuchi Akiyoshi and Fukuda Shin'ichi [1987] "Nihon no mainbank wa dono yohna yakuwari wo hatashitaka" (What was the role of the Japanese main bank system?), Nihon Ginko Kinyu Kenkyujo *Kinyu Kenkyu* 6 (3): 1–28.

Horiuchi Akiyoshi and Okazaki Ryoko [1992] "Capital Markets and the Banking Sector: The Efficiency of Japanese Banks in Reducing Agency Costs," Discussion Paper 92-F-6 Research Institute for the Japanese Economy, Faculty of Economics, University of Tokyo.

Horiuchi Akiyoshi, F. Packer and S. Fukuda [1988] "What Role Has the Main Bank Played in Japan?," *Journal of the Japanese and International Economies*, 2: 159–80.

Hoshi Takeo, A. Kashyap and D. Scharfstein [1990a] "Bank Monitoring and Investment: Evidence from the Changing Structure of Japanese Corporate Banking Relationships," in R. Glenn Hubbard (ed.) *Asymmetric Information, Corporate Finance, and Economic Development*, 105–26. Chicago: University of Chicago Press.

Hoshi Takeo, A. Kashyap and D. Scharfstein [1990b] "The Role of Banks in Reducing Costs of Financial Distress in Japan," *Journal of Financial Economics*, 27: 67–88.

— [1991] "Corporate Structure, Liquidity, and Investment: Evidence from Japanese Industrial Groups," *Quarterly Journal of Economics*, 106: 33–60.

Ikeo Kazuhito [1993] "Kinyu no micro-keizaigaku—kabushiki mochiai" (Microeconomics of cross-shareholding), *Keizai Seminar*, Nihon Hyoronsha, March.

Imai Ken'ichi [1990] "The Legitimacy of Japan's Corporate Groups," *Japan Echo*, 3: 23–8.

Ishino Iwao [1953] "The *Oyabun-Kobun*: A Japanese Ritual Kinship Institution," *American Anthropology* #55.

Ito Kunio [1993] "Kabushiki mochiai: sono rasenkei 'logic' " (Cross-Shareholding: A Spiral Logic), in T. Itami, T. Kagono and M. Ito (eds) *Nihon no Kigyo System: Dai-ichi kan—Kigyo to Nani-ka* (Japanese Enterprise System: Series 1—What is an enterprise?). Tokyo: Yushikaku Publishing.

Japan Economic Planning Agency [1992] *White Paper: Economic Survey of Japan, 1991–92*. Tokyo.

Japan Fair Trade Commission [1989] *Kigyo shudan no jittai ni tsuite* (On the status of the enterprise groups). Tokyo.

Jensen, Michael C. and William H. Meckling [1976] "Theory of the Firm: Managerial Behavior, Agency Costs and Ownership Structure," *Journal of Financial Economics*, 3: 305–60.

Jick, Todd D. [1979] "Mixing Qualitative and Quantitative Methods: Triangulation in Action," *Administrative Science Quarterly*, 24: 602–11.

Johnson, Chalmers [1982] *MITI and the Japanese Miracle*. Stanford, CA: Stanford University Press.

Kanesaki Yoshitasu [1986] "Kabushiki mochiai ga aru baai-no kigyo kachi to CAPM" (Cross-shareholding's effect on the value of the enterprise and the Capital Asset Pricing Model), *Finansu Kenkyu*, no. 5.

Kang Jun-Koo and Anil Shivdasani [1995] "Firm Performance, Corporate Governance, and Top Executive Turnover in Japan," *Journal of Financial Economics*, 38: 29–58.

Kaplan, Steven N. and Bernadette A. Minton [1994] "Appointments of Outsiders to Japanese Boards: Determinants and Implications for Managers,"*Journal of Financial Economics*, 36: 225–58.

Kawakita Hidetaka [1992] "Kigyo zaimu wo mushibamu 104 choen no kabushiki mochiai" (¥104 trillion of cross-held shares eat away at company fiscal management), *Kinyu Zaisei Jijo*, Oct. 12: 40–4.

— [1993] "Kabushiki antei hoyu no keisei to genjo" (The present situation of maintaining stable shareholdings), Shadanhojin Nippon Shoken Anaristu Kyokai. *Shoken Anaristu Janaru*, June.

Kobayashi Takao [1991] "Kabushiki no jukyu to kabuka" parts 1–6 (The supply and demand of stocks and stock prices), Yasashii Keizaigaku *Nihon Keizai Shimbun*, July 12–18.

— [1992] "Kabushiki mochiai to kabuka" (Cross-shareholdings and stock prices) *Gendai shoken jiten* (Dictionary of Contemporary Securities) Nippon Shoken Keizai Kenkyujo-hen.

Kumagai Goro [1994] "Kabushiki shisan wa ROA jo, ALM jo asshuku sareru beki mono da" (ROA and ALM data require a cap on stock investments) *Kinyu Zaisei Jijo*, Sept. 12: 32–6.

Kurasawa Sukenari [1984] "Kabushiki mochiai to kigyo kachi" (Cross-shareholding and the value of an enterprise). *Finansu Kenkyu*, no. 2.

Lawler, Edward E. [1985] "Challenging Traditional Research Assumptions," in E. Lawler *et al. Doing Research That Is Useful for Theory and Practice*. San Francisco: Jossey-Bass.

Mabuchi Haru [1993] *NRC Toshi Geppo*, November. Tokyo: Nikko Research Center Ltd.

Matsumoto Yoshiharu [1960] "Contemporary Japan, The Individual and the Group," *Transactions of the American Philosophical Society*, New Series–vol. 50, part I.

Merton, Robert K., M.O. Fiske and Patricia Kendall [1956] *The Focused Interview*. New York: Free Press.

Mintzberg, Henry [1979] "An Emerging Strategy of 'Direct Research,'" *Administrative Science Quarterly*, 24: 580–9.

Mito Tadashi [1992] "'Ie no ronri' to Nihon shakai (2): keiyaku-gata to shozoku-gata—zangyo to tetsudai" ('Logic of *Ie*' and Japanese Society (part 2): Contract-model versus Belonging-model—Overtime work and helping-out), *Shosai no Mado*, 3: 4–10.

Mitsui Gomei-Kaisha [1933] *The House of Mitsui, A Record of Three Centuries: Past History and Present Enterprises*. Tokyo: Mitsui Gomei-Kaisha.

Miwa Yoshiro [1985] "Mainbank to sono kinou" (The Function of Main Banks), in Y. Kosai and S. Nishikawa (eds) *Nihon Keizai Sistemu* 170–99. Tokyo: University of Tokyo Press

— [1991] "Mainbank to Nihon no shihon shijo" (Main banks and Japanese capital markets), Zenginkyo *Kin'yu*, August: 11–19.

Miyajima Hideaki [1994] "The Transformation of *Zaibatsu* to Postwar Corporate Groups—From Hierarchically Integrated Groups to Horizontally Integrated Groups," *Journal of the Japanese and International Economies*, 8: 293–328.

Miyamoto Matao [1984] "The Position and Role of Family Business in the Development of the Japanese Company System," in A. Okochi and S. Yasuoka (eds) *Family Business in the Era of Industrial Growth, Its Ownership and Management*, 39–91. Tokyo: University of Tokyo Press.

Nakagawa Kei'ichiro [1977] *Social Order and Entrepreneurship*. Tokyo: University of Tokyo Press.

Nakane Chie [1970] *Japanese Society*. Berkeley and Los Angeles: University of California Press.

— [1990] "Tokugawa Society," in C. Nakane and S. Oishi (eds) *Tokugawa Japan, The Social and Economic Antecedents of Modern Japan*, 213–31. Tokyo: University of Tokyo Press.

Nakatani Iwao [1983] "Kigyo shudan no keizaiteki imi to ginko no yakuwari" (The economic significance of the enterprise groups and the role of banks), *Kin'yu Keizai,* 202: 51–75.

— [1984] "The Economic Role of Financial Corporate Grouping," in M. Aoki (ed.) *The Economic Analysis of the Japanese Firm,* 227–58. North-Holland: Elsevier Publishing.

— [1990] "Opening Up Fortress Japan," *Japan Echo.* 3: 8–11.

Nishiguchi Toshihiro [1992] *Strategic Industrial Sourcing.* London: Oxford University Press.

Noguchi Yukio [1995] *1940-nen taisei: saraba "senji keizai"* (The 1940s system: farewell to the "wartime economy"), Tokyo: Toyo Keizai Shinposha.

Nomura Sogo Kenkyujo [1992] "Nihon kigyo no corporate governance" (Corporate governance of Japanese companies), *Zaikai Kansoku,* September.

Oba Ryoko and Horiuchi Akiyoshi [1991] "Honpo kigyo no mainbank kankei to setsubi toshi kodo no kankei ni tsuite" (On the relationship between our country's corporate main bank system and capital expenditure behavior). Nihon Ginko Kinyu Kenkyujo *Kinyu Kenkyu,* 9 (4): 23–50, December.

Ogishima Seiji [1993] "Kabushiki mochiai ga kabuka keisei ni ateru eikyo" (The influence of cross-shareholding upon stock prices), Shadanhojin Nippon Shoken Anaristu Kyokai. *Shoken Anaristu Janaru,* June.

Okazaki Ryoko and Horiuchi Akiyoshi [1992] "Kigyo no setsubi toshi to mainbank kankei" (The relationship between the main bank and corporate capital expenditure). Nihon Ginko Kinyu Kenkyujo *Kinyu Kenkyu* 11 (1): 37–59 (March).

Okazaki Tetsuji [1994] "The Japanese Firm Under the Wartime Planned Economy," in M. Aoki and R. Dore (eds) *The Japanese Firm, Sources of Competitive Strength.* Oxford: Oxford University Press.

Okochi Akio and Yasuoka Shigeaki (eds) [1984] *Family Business in the Era of Industrial Growth, Its Ownership and Management.* Tokyo: University of Tokyo Press.

Okumura Hiroshi [1990a] "Intercorporate Relations in Japan," *Ryukoki Daigaku Keizai Keiei Ronso,* 29(4): 21–8 (March).

— [1990b] *Kigyo baishu—M&A no jidai* (Company buyouts in the M&A era). Tokyo: Iwanami Shoten.

— [1991] "The Roots of the Securities Scam," *Japan Echo,* 18 (4): 16–22.

— [1993] "Shareholders' Rights a Joke!," *Tokyo Business Today.* October 20–21.

Omura Kei'ichi [1993] *Kabushiki mochiai no ishiki kozo* (How companies consider cross-shareholding), Report of International Finance Group, Keiei Academy, Tokyo.

Ouchi, William G. [1980] "Markets, Bureaucracies, and Clans," *Administrative Science Quarterly,* March: 129–41.

— [1981] *Theory Z: How American Business Can Meet the Japanese Challenge.* Reading, MA: Addison-Wesley.

Patrick, Hugh [1967] "Japan 1886–1914," in Rondo Cameron (ed.) *Banking in the Early Stages of Industrialization: A Study of Comparative Economic History*. New York: Oxford University Press.

— [1983] "Japanese Financial Development in Historical Perspective" in Gustav Ranis *et al.* (eds) *Comparative Development Perspectives*. Boulder, CO: Westview Press.

— [1994] "The Relevance of Japanese Finance and Its Main Bank System," in M. Aoki and H. Patrick (eds) *The Japanese Main Bank System: Its Relevancy for Developing and Transforming Economies*. Oxford: Oxford University Press.

Pelzel, John C. [1970] "Japanese Kinship: A Comparison," in Maurice Freedman (ed.) *Family and Kinship in Chinese Society*. Stanford, CA: Stanford University Press.

Pitelis, Christos [1995] "From Transaction Costs Economics to Thesmoeconomics," paper presented, 12th EGOS Colloquium, Istanbul.

Putterman, Louis [1988] "The Firm as Association Versus the Firm as Commodity: Efficiency, Rights, and Ownership," *Economics and Philosophy*, 4: 243–66.

Sakakibara Eisuke [1994] *Beyond Capitalism: The Japanese Model of Market Economics*. Lanham, MD: University Press of America/Economic Strategy Institute.

Sako Mari [1992] *Prices, Quality and Trust: Inter-firm Relations in Britain and Japan*. Cambridge: Cambridge University Press.

Sakudo Yotaro [1990] "The Management Practices of Family Business," in C. Nakane and S. Oishi (ed.) *Tokugawa Japan, The Social and Economic Antecedents of Modern Japan*, 147–166. Tokyo: University of Tokyo Press.

Sansom, George B. [1950] *The Western World and Japan*. New York: Alfred A. Knopf Publishers.

Schaede, Ulrike [1993] "Understanding Corporate Governance in Japan: Do Classical Concepts Apply?," CCC Working Paper No. 93-12, Center for Research in Management, Univ. California at Berkeley.

— [1994] "Corporate Governance in Japan: Institutional Investors, Management Monitoring and Corporate Stakeholders," *Industrial and Corporate Change*, 2: 285–323.

Scher, Mark J. [1993] "The Main Bank Relationship: An Empirical Look at Profitability and Practice," paper presented at Annual Meeting of Association for Japanese Business Studies, Vancouver, January 1994.

Scher, Mark J. and P. Ciancanelli [1993] "Families, Firms and Collectivity: Japanese Business Organization in Historical Perspective," *Best Paper Proceedings*, Sixth Annual Meeting of the Association for Japanese Business Studies, New York. January 1993: 231–7.

Sheard, Paul [1989] "The Main Bank System and Corporate Monitoring and Control in Japan," *Journal of Economic Behavior*, 11: 399–422.

— [1991] "The Economics of Interlocking Shareholding," *Ricerche Economiche*, 45: 421–48.

— [1994a] "Reciprocal Delegated Monitoring in the Japanese Main Bank System," *Journal of the Japanese and International Economies*, 8 (1): 1–21.

Sheard, Paul [1994b] "Interlocking Shareholdings and Corporate Governance," in M. Aoki and R. Dore (eds) *The Japanese Firm, Sources of Competitive Strength*. Oxford: Oxford University Press.

— [1994c] "Bank Executives on Japanese Corporate Boards," *Bank of Japan Monetary and Economic Studies*, 12 (2): 85–121.

— [1994d] "Main Banks and the Governance of Financial Distress," in M. Aoki and H. Patrick (eds) *The Japanese Main Bank System: Its Relevancy for Developing and Transforming Economies*. Oxford: Oxford University Press.

Teranishi Juro [1994] "Loan Syndication in War-Time Japan and the Origins of the Main Bank System," in M. Aoki and H. Patrick (eds) *The Japanese Main Bank System: Its Relevancy for Developing and Transforming Economies*. Oxford: Oxford University Press.

Wakasugi Keimei [1982] "Kabushiki mochiai no zaimuteki igi" (The financial significance of cross-shareholding) in *Nipponteki keiei zaimu no kaimei* (Views of Japanese treasurers) by Nippon Keiei Zaimu Kenkyu Gakkai-hen. Chuo Keizai-sha.

Weber, Max [1921/1947] (*Wirtschaft und Gesellschaft*) *The Theory of Social and Economic Organization*. Translated by A.M. Henderson and Talcott Parsons. Edited with an Introduction by T. Parsons, 1947. New York: Oxford University Press.

Whitley, Richard [1992] *Business Systems in East Asia: Firms Markets and Societies*. London: Sage Publications.

Williamson, Oliver E. [1975] *Markets and Hierarchies: Analysis and Antitrust Implications*. New York: Free Press.

— [1985] *The Economic Institutions of Capitalism: Firms, Markets and Relational Contracting*. New York: Free Press.

Yasuoka Shigeaki [1984] "Capital Ownership in Family Companies: Japanese Firms Compared with Those in Other Countries," in A. Okochi and S. Yasuoka (eds) *Family Business in the Era of Industrial Growth, Its Ownership and Management*, 1–32. Tokyo: University of Tokyo Press.

Yin, Robert K. [1984] *Case Study Research*. Beverly Hills, CA: Sage Publications.

Yonekura Seiichiro [1985] "The Emergence of the Prototype of Enterprise Group Capitalism—The Case of Mitsui," *Hitotsubashi Journal of Commerce and Management*, 20 (December): 63–104.

Yoshino M.Y. [1968] *Japan's Managerial System, Tradition and Innovation*. Cambridge, MA: MIT Press.

Yoshino Toshihiko [1977] "The Creation of the Bank of Japan—Its Western Origin and Adaptation," *The Developing Economies*, 3: 381–401.

Zenkoku Shoken Torihikijo Kyogikai [1992] *Kabushiki bunpu jokyo chosa* (Survey of the state of share distribution). Tokyo.

Index